# Escorting the Monarch

*For all those who have served in the SEG,*
*civilian and police, especially my dad*

# Escorting the Monarch

## The Story of the Metropolitan Police's 'Special Escort Group'

Chris Jagger

Foreword by HRH Prince Michael of Kent

PEN & SWORD HISTORY

First published in Great Britain in 2017
by Pen & Sword History
An imprint of Pen & Sword Books Limited
47 Church Street
Barnsley
South Yorkshire
S70 2AS

Copyright © Chris Jagger 2017

ISBN 978 1 52672 041 2

The right of Chris Jagger to be identified as
Author of this Work has been asserted by him in accordance
with the Copyright, Designs and Patents Act 1988.

A CIP catalogue record for this book is
available from the British Library

Typeset in Ehrhardt
by Mac Style Ltd, Bridlington, East Yorkshire

Printed and bound in the UK
by CPI Group (UK) Ltd, Croydon, CR0 4YY

Pen & Sword Books Limited incorporates the imprints of Atlas,
Archaeology, Aviation, Discovery, Family History, Fiction, History,
Maritime, Military, Military Classics, Politics, Select, Transport,
True Crime, Air World, Frontline Publishing, Leo Cooper,
Remember When, Seaforth Publishing, The Praetorian Press,
Wharncliffe Local History, Wharncliffe Transport,
Wharncliffe True Crime and White Owl

For a complete list of Pen & Sword titles please contact
PEN & SWORD BOOKS LIMITED
47 Church Street, Barnsley, South Yorkshire, S70 2AS, England
E-mail: enquiries@pen-and-sword.co.uk
Website: www.pen-and-sword.co.uk

# Contents

# Acknowledgements

Escorting the Monarch wouldn't exist if it weren't for the support I was offered by family, friends and fellow collaborators. A big thank you to my dad, David Jagger, for priming me with stories as a child, bringing me to work as a teen, and for not already writing the book, therefore leaving the task to me. My mum believed I was the correct person to write the book, and encouraged me to quiz my dad and squeeze him for the foundations on which to do my research. My Icelandic family provided me with the grounds on which to build. They created the space and time I needed to research, think and write. My wife, Gerdur Bjork Kjaernested, was my biggest cheerleader, most ruthless editor, and my wisest second pair of eyes. The acknowledgements couldn't pass without recognition of my brilliant border collie Embla. She listened to my frustrations, barked at my opposition, kept loyal to my point of view, and sat close by my side, often on my feet, through hours of reading and writing. Then there were my friends, the people who kept asking me questions about the group, and listened to endless tedious accounts about the book's progress, especially Christopher Mole, Jakob Thor Kristiansson, Jamie Kaye and Gudmundur Ingolfsson.

But it's the collaborators we must all offer our widest thanks to. For they're the ones who dug deep to recall distant memories on which the book is based. They accepted the burden of my endless questions, and shared their stories, thoughts and ideas. Some of them were entirely unsuspecting members of the public who happened to be positions of interest to me, such as the Director of the Churchill Archives or the grandson of a former President of Iceland. Many others had served with the SEG, or were members of their family. In working with me, my fellow collaborators led me make a public record of the group's history – for that I am eternally grateful. John Gouldsmith, Gerry Mobbs, Brian Toon, Tony Dolan, Steve Brownridge, Jill Preedy, Rick Johnson, Martin Vaisey, David Prout, Eugiene Brooks and Jim

Read are but a few. There are of course too many contributors to name, but special thanks must be given to Bob Stewart for his encouragement, insights and enthusiasm. Philip Williams for causing me to think deeply, and appreciate the unique innovation in the work of the SEG. Colin and Liz Tebbutt for trusting in me, believing in the book and for showing me the more personal and nuanced side of the security business. Through years of chats, laughs and stories, Colin Tebbutt showed me the unique human skills and personal discipline needed to be to be an effective bodyguard. John Swain for giving me the occasional push, and for helping so diligently behind the scenes. Martyn Hillier for teaching me about motorcycles. Trevor Pryke for putting me on the right track – many times – and Peter Skerritt for helping me imagine myself as one of the motorcycle escorts. Also Andrew Cooper (technical drawings of bikes) and Lt. Colonel Chris Topham (sketches).

Thank you to the photographers Bill Scott, Ian Davidson and Bullshire Police, for their wonderful photos.

I'm especially grateful to Jessica Bangs and her mother Diane Davis, grandchild and daughter of the late Jock Shields (SEG) for helping me get to know one of the key influencers in groups history.

Then there is the very fine team at Pen and Sword. Thank you for giving me gentle direction, for casting your magic on my manuscript, but mostly for giving me the opportunity, and the freedom, to write the group's story as I saw fit. But my greatest thanks are reserved to a man who sadly won't be able to read the book – the late John Baldwin, from whom I gained so much inspiration.

# Preface

Some of my earliest and fondest memories are of my dad dressed from head to toe in police motorcycle uniform and white crash helmet. I was lucky, unlike my two older brothers who shared a room at the back of our north London house looking out over our garden and Grovelands Park, my room sat above the front door, which meant I had a view over the street. Some mornings I'd wake up very early at the sound of the front door closing, normally around 5.00 am. I'd climb out of bed and sneak a look through the bedroom curtains listening carefully for the sound of the garage door opening. The next thing I'd hear was the sound of my dad's motorcycle firing up – a sudden electric whizz shortly followed by a smooth burst of power. The bike, a gleaming white BMW boxer, sounded like a cross between a spaceship from one of my brother's Star Trek movies and a purring lion. As my dad rode the bike up the driveway I'd close the gap in the curtains in case he looked up so he wouldn't catch me watching. He'd then turn left, into the street, facing uphill, and slowly pull away, soon vanishing out of view. It was one of the coolest things ever. But what did he actually do?

As I grew a little older and ever so slightly more trustworthy, my dad would occasionally take me to work with him in the car. We'd visit the garage in Barnes, a fancy residential area in south-west London, a stone's throw from the River Thames. Going there was always exciting and felt like a real privilege. The journey to Barnes was navigated through various back streets and shortcuts often passing by some of London's wealthiest neighbourhoods, most beautiful buildings, fanciest houses and biggest inner-city parks. Somehow Dad always managed to avoid the other traffic; we rarely met a red light and hardly ever needed to touch the brakes. Looking out the car window I was in awe. We normally followed a route from our north London suburb up through Barnet, Finchley, Hampstead, Swiss Cottage and then across the very impressive green and gold embossed Hammersmith Bridge. Crossing that bridge felt like entering into the world of royalty.

The garage was hidden down a quiet residential street. Upstairs housed the office, locker and staff room and a number of mysterious 'no-go' rooms. I was free to wander about and spent much of the time distracting my dad from his job and trying to get him to play with me on one of the rarely-used full-size snooker tables. There was also a huge TV, much bigger than the one we had at home. It was normally surrounded by half a dozen or so blokes in motorcycle kit drinking tea, telling jokes, throwing paper planes and half-heartedly watching the news.

The long corridor between the offices and locker rooms was home to dozens of important-looking plaques, together with photos of my dad and his colleagues lined up with their police motorcycles. Many of the photos were of the Special Escort Group (SEG) and personal protection officers together with various members of the royal family. One of those photos was of a royal prince sitting on top of a SEG motorcycle. In some of the offices there were complicated-looking maps of London posted on the walls covered in tiny coloured flags and handwritten sticky notes. In the background you could hear the crackling of police radios, slamming of locker doors and the buzzing of pagers and telephones. The office had an air of great importance but shared it with a lively, friendly, fun atmosphere.

Then there was the basement. This was where the real action happened. This was what the garage was all about. This was also where I couldn't believe my dad would let me hang out unsupervised and free to do as I wished. There I was, about 12-years-old, fascinated by sirens and switches and surrounded by scores of immaculately clean and shiny police BMW motorcycles, Range Rovers, SD1 Rovers and even the occasional Rolls Royce. Feeling like a royal prince, I'd sit on my dad's bike, flicking buttons, pulling important-looking knobs and 'accidentally' pressing the horn, as trios of my dad's colleagues would pass by on their bikes, riding up the ramp on to the street and out of the garage, often waving to me as they launched off. This was cool, very cool indeed.

Inspired by my dad's career, some seven years later I found myself going through the recruitment process to become a civilian employee of the Metropolitan Police Service. I was very fortunate to start out at New

Scotland Yard in a position that gave me an excellent insight into all aspects of police work. I left the police some years later to work with the Home Office continuing in the field of security. Much of my time has been spent living and working overseas for Her Majesty's Government, the United Nations as well as NATO (North Atlantic Treaty Organization). During this time, I've been very fortunate to have worked closely with a handful of talented teams from across the military and police as well as national security and intelligence agencies from around the world. Many were impressive, but none come close to matching the *esprit de corps* of the SEG.

Researching and writing this book has been a pleasure and in part has been an opportunity for me to relive elements of my childhood. Furthermore, having spent much of my own career thus far in the field of security it has been fascinating to study such a specialist and famous team. They have mastered the art of making something that ought to be impossible look easy to the casual observer. One of the greatest challenges in writing the book has been to convey the complexity, skill and precision of what they do to you, the reader. I hope I have done the SEG justice.

To the very best of my investigatory efforts, I have sought to unearth the facts that help tell their story. In doing so, the investigation took me far and wide. Sadly, some facts appear to have been lost, hidden beyond reach or, frustratingly and rather simply, unknowable. Very few official archives pertaining to the SEG have been kept by the Metropolitan Police, so a number of historical facts and figures are absent; however, I have faith that those which could be discovered have been and were carefully used to underpin this book.

A significant part of my research was interview based, and I am especially thankful to all who shared their stories with me. Many of those I interviewed said that their SEG days were the best of their career. I'm not surprised. I should imagine this is partly due to the unique and exciting nature of their work, but mostly because of an incredible team spirit and camaraderie that has built up over the six decades of their history.

Each chapter tells a story of how the group has evolved in response to hard work, opportunity, ingenuity and an ever-changing, complex and dangerous security environment. I focus on a small number of SEG officers who feature as particularly important to the development of the group. There are many others, known and unknown to myself, who are equally important, but I have been unable to mention. Yet it should be known that no single step, leap or jump in their story was achieved as an individual act. The SEG is a team, a family. Those unnamed individuals, and their families, should understand that their contribution was no less important.

Due to the sensitive nature of their work some aspects of their story will remain untold. Protecting the good work of the SEG has always been my priority; henceforth content has been edited accordingly. Interviews were frank and responses even franker, but details that could in any way disadvantage the group on the grounds of trust, confidentiality or operational security were omitted. For a host of reasons some of the officers who contributed memories towards the book remain anonymous. All of those who helped were encouraged to share their thoughts on the book's final content. Their help, guidance and encouragement will forever be appreciated.

Finally, I hope you enjoy reading this book as much as I enjoyed researching and writing it. Long may the SEG continue to make such important history.

Chris Jagger, author of the SEG's history

# Introduction

by Chief Superintendent John Baldwin
(Longest-serving Chief of SEG)

My years in the SEG, or the 'group' as I used to call us, made up many of the fondest in my career. Following a short but active career with the Royal Engineers, I left the army in late 1947, and proudly joined the Metropolitan Police in January 1948. At the newly-promoted rank of Sergeant, I took over the SEG and became its first dedicated and full time leader in 1960. I'm extremely proud to say that I was able to stay with the group and help it grow for 13 years of my police career; rising from Sergeant to Chief Superintendent, and always leading from the saddle of my bike.

As this history will explain, the idea for the SEG was born in the preparations of the visit of Tito in 1953. These preparations not only mark the first of their kind since the end of the war, but also the first to use a police motorcycle escort – a great honour and new responsibility for the Metropolitan Police.

As you will see from the images on the following pages of this book, the original group of officers that formed the SEG understood the importance of underpinning their methods with perfect precision and polished presentation. This approach ensured the VIP would arrive on time, safely and in a style befitting to their rank and position.

The first motorcycle escort I was responsible for leading was for the President of Cameroon along with a number of his government advisors when they attended what became known as the 'London Talks' in 1960. Perhaps one of the most important milestones for the group was reached at the funeral of Sir. Winston Churchill. No less than 60 Kings, Queens and Heads of State were expected to attend the ceremony at St Paul's Cathedral and the SEG were charged to ensure they arrived safely, in a way fitting to the ceremony, and perhaps most importantly, exactly on time; not a moment too early or too late. From the perspective of the police and the primary organisers, the event was a flawless success. Within the Metropolitan Police's own ranks the group secured the support it needed to grow. We had proven our ability as a world-class escort group. It has been an absolute pleasure to observe the SEG continue to grow from strength to strength over the last six decades.

I truly hope you enjoy reading their story.

# Foreword

## by HRH Prince Michael of Kent

*This is an opportunity for me to commend the professionalism and long experience of the Special Escort Group. I have had the privilege of their assistance from time to time over many years. They are far better trained than any similar organisation in foreign countries, and bring to their work a combination of firmness and friendliness which is admirable. In contrast here are some incidents from my own experience which illustrate this:*

*I remember a police motorcyclist in Swaziland who picked up with his foot, as he went along, the hat a workman had put on the ground beside him, and drove with the hat impaled on his foot all the way back to Government House, where he proudly showed off the miserable garment, now past its prime.*

*And there was the police motorcyclist in the Caribbean who weaved from side to side as he drove along in front of me, and later explained that his helmet was fitted with music and that he was listening to the latest reggae number.*

*In the Middle East I once had a police car escort which, on joining a motorway from the slip road, immediately swung out into the outside lane straight in front of another car which ran into the back of it. We never saw the police car, or its occupants, again, although they were apparently unharmed.*

*And in St Petersburg in Russia a police car was leading me to an important road safety meeting when he shot a red light and drove full tilt into some unfortunate car going across his bows and carried straight on without bothering to check on the condition of the occupants.*

*All these incidents were, incidentally, witnessed by my own protection officers sitting in the car with me. And they made me appreciate the work of the SEG in the most convincing way.*

*They manage to manoeuvre through the densest traffic, and display the utmost courtesy to other drivers who may have been inconvenienced. Their knowledge of all the highways and byways of London is encyclopaedic and would put even a taxi-driver to shame. Their expertise deserves to be made available to all other police forces worldwide.*

*I wish the Group every success now and in the future.*

*HRH Prince Michael of Kent*

# Introduction from the Author

The Special Escort Group (SEG) has been honing its skills for over six decades. Developing an unequivocal team culture dedicated to absolute precision, it has a reputation for excellence amongst its peers, of delivering its passengers (and cargo) on time, safely, in a great deal of style, and without fuss or mishap. The group is neither shaken nor stirred. Thrown into the deep end from the outset it has become the world leader in its specialist role. Affectionately known to much of the British public as 'the Queen's bodyguards', the group has gained high levels of public admiration over the years.

The SEG story carries with it a scent of engine oil and polish. Although its work demands exquisitely high levels of presentation, there is little room for gloss or glitter. It is instructed with safeguarding individuals and property that require the highest possible levels of protection. The trust bestowed upon the group could not be greater. From queens, kings, presidents and emperors, to priceless works of art, terrorists and high-risk prisoners, SEG escorts them all. The skill required to protect them demands a world-class team.

The group's officers put their lives on the line every day. The risks are understandably high, not only from the possibility of an adversary attacking the motorcade, but also from the potential of a serious road traffic accident. Most of the runs take place in central London during the busiest times of day. The motorcycle outriders perform their function at high speed; riding rapidly between junctions, often negotiating heavy and unpredictable traffic conditions, navigating through tight-moving gaps, sometimes against oncoming traffic. The convoy itself usually comprises a single VIP limousine, closely followed by an SEG Range Rover. Led by a single motorcycle, known as the 'easy rider', the vehicles glide and weave elegantly through the momentary gaps created by the motorcycle escorts. It is the highly-honed skills of this group of experienced officers that keep the VIP, the public and its own team safe.

The task of protecting our nation's royal family and visiting heads of state has been undertaken by only a small number of individuals over the centuries. Those who carry this charge are trusted to perform to the highest possible standards, and it has always been that way; from the horse-mounted outriders that escorted the monarchy in the twelfth century to the sophisticated security teams that protect HMQ (Her Majesty the Queen) today. The SEG is not only the first police motorcycle protection team of its kind in the world; it is also the most admired. This is the SEG's story.

## A Day in the Life of the Special Escort Group

To assist readers in gaining an impression of what the job of an SEG officer entails, for a few brief, heart-pounding moments, I would like to invite you to participate in a routine escort.

If you've spent any time at all in central London, the chances are you've seen them at work. If you haven't, you've missed out. Assuming you have, then you'll immediately understand why I use the words 'elegance', 'skill', 'confidence' and 'precision' to describe them. Like a flock of upright, alert, proud and ever so slightly regal swans, a group convoy glides seemingly without effort through busy London. The vehicles move gracefully whilst the motorcycle outriders stride out at much greater speed, sashaying junction to junction, through the most congested city in the United Kingdom.

*Your part is important as there is no room for redundancy in this team. You're a newly-appointed member of this elite and prestigious group. Experienced police officer, fifteen years service, enthusiastic motorcyclist, you have become a member of the group and it's a professional dream come true. Almost six months of tutoring and training will have seen you tested and evaluated by your colleagues on well over 100 routine jobs. On a busy day, you will participate in multiple escorts, switching between riding specially-designed motorcycles and driving powerful cars. The more experienced of your colleagues will be involved in as many as five escorts in a single day. Today you climb onto the saddle of a highly-polished, finely-tuned motorcycle. It's a beautiful machine adapted from the original factory set-up for its unique tasks in the SEG.*

*Your role today is that of motorcycle 'outrider' – a description favoured by the press but one that gives little clue to the actual part you will play. The main job of the outrider, or more accurately 'escort', is to ensure that the route ahead is clear and safe for the following convoy. You create the gaps in which the needle and thread will weave. You do this by calmly powering ahead, overtaking moving traffic, manoeuvring into gaps and quickly pausing in highly visible positions – momentarily stopping traffic and people at busy junctures. Exceptional concentration and confident motorcycling skills are needed to achieve this with safety and precision.*

*You capture the attention of everyone with a combination of bike positioning, staccato blows on your whistle and by directing the actions with clear and unambiguous hand signals. It seems like only a few seconds until the convoy approaches and floats through. As it moves away from the juncture, one of your fellow escorts has already launched ahead at speed to begin controlling the next obstacle. Once the convoy is clear your final job is to thank those you've temporarily interrupted with a nod, smile and a wave. You then power up to move swiftly to the next stoppage. The technique, often delivered by three or more escort motorcycles, is known as leapfrogging.*

*This isn't your first escort, but it is the first time you will have escorted HMQ. You know she's to be collected from Buckingham Palace but, for security reasons, you've not yet been told what her destination will be. Over the previous months, you have demonstrated a near-perfect record of runs so your team skipper has decided it's time to escort the Monarch. As is normal practice on many escorts, and for security reasons, you only discover that you are to escort the Queen at the very last moment. You've trained hard for this day but a run with Her Majesty will set the butterflies off for sure.*

*You are about to leave the basement garage at SEG HQ, together with three of your colleagues who are also on motorcycles. The Range Rover will be following closely behind. The powerful and heavily-adapted vehicle contains three more of your colleagues who are ready to provide uniformed assistance in an emergency. You are well-rehearsed and trained to work closely together. With weapons, radios and other essential equipment checked, the controller announces that the team is ready to proceed.*

*Your bike is beautifully presented – spotless and gleaming. It had better be following nearly two hours of meticulous cleaning and polishing. Capable of reaching high speed in a single twist of the wrist, you mindfully pull away from the garage, climb up the steep exit ramp and into a leafy residential street in central London. Pride, excitement and confidence in your ability all wash over you in those first seconds as you reflect on the past months. Training in all-weather conditions, hours of soap followed by layers of polish and the repeated practice of escorting techniques all led to you becoming a member of this team. But now's not the time to dwell on where you've been. You remind yourself of your training, as what you're about to do requires calm and committed concentration.*

*As you pull out into a busy main road your teammates manoeuvre behind you forming what looks like an arrowhead if seen from above. Tightly held together and spaced equally apart, the precision and locked movement catches the attention of onlookers. A child walking to school with her father stops and waves as you pass them by. You offer a friendly nod in their direction. You notice in the mirrors of your bike that your likeminded colleagues have done the same. The gesture brings a smile to your face.*

*With an eye on the clock, you are now 'exactly' ten minutes into your journey to Buckingham Palace from your London base. Communication between you and your colleagues has been kept to a minimum save for one or two bad jokes about your motorcycling skills from the control vehicle following closely behind. I say exactly because timing to the second is essential in this job. 'Royals run to time and so should you' – these words from an experienced training buddy ring loud and clear in your mind.*

*As with most Monday mornings, traffic is heavy. Today though is particularly congested. A significant part of London's main inner circular road, the A406, is restricted to a single lane due to roadworks. Unusually for a Monday morning, an unannounced political demonstration is taking place outside the Houses of Parliament with an estimated 5,000 protesters in attendance. The crowd has caused Whitehall to be closed temporarily. This is combined with a serious traffic accident, which has closed off the Swiss Cottage part of the Finchley Road for several hours. The knock-on effect has caused an increase in traffic jams in central London and many of the morning commuters have grown impatient.*

*During the short time that you've been on the move you've observed scores of potential hazards from pedestrians and traffic and you've countered them by adjusting your road speed and road position. You're an expert at reading and predicting traffic. Although your VIP is not yet in convoy, practising this level of observation is essential as it keeps you sharp and maintains your mental habits for when you'll need them most. Good observation means you can react quickly, accurately and calmly. Honing your reactions as best you can in this job helps keep everyone safe.*

*You navigate around bustling Trafalgar Square and pass through the imposing Admiralty Arch. In the distance, you see Buckingham Palace. Despite reminding yourself this escort is just like any other, you can't help but start to feel excited. Very few individuals have had the privilege of escorting the Monarch and now you're going to go down in SEG history as one of them.*

*The gates of the palace begin to open, timed perfectly with your arrival. Your teammates conduct another communications test before manoeuvring into the predetermined waiting area of the quadrangle where the daily Changing of the Guard takes place. Your arrival is carried out with an appropriate level of ceremony, attention to detail and, once again, precision. There's another reminder from one of your teammates, this time across the radio: 'If you put the wrong foot down and tread on my shiny boots I will be very unhappy.'*

*With measured care and very little effort, each of the three motorbikes has lined up next to one another; in identical postures, in perfect symmetry, spaced equally apart, with each of the front wheels on the edge of the same line of the pavement turned neatly to the left. Glancing down at your front wheel you notice that the brand name of the tyre – 'Dunlop' – which sits embossed on the rim, has been hand painted in gold. Looking across at the other motorcycles you see that they are all the same. The teammate closest to you notices what's caught your eye and explains that one of the officers on the other relief had the idea of painting the lettering gold for extra effect. He was right: it looks great. The Range Rover has gently come to rest behind you.*

*The brief wait is followed by a small number of royal household staff gathering at the door from which HMQ will depart. One of her cars, a Phantom Rolls Royce in claret livery, gently draws up and aligns itself adjacent to a red carpet that extends from the pavement to the palace. You and your teammates catch a wave from the chauffeur. He is a rather small chap, with the stature of a racing jockey, immaculately turned out in his uniform. You have met him before on various driver training and bodyguard courses.*

*A few more quiet moments pass before you get the nod that HMQ is about to emerge. She does so walking purposely towards you – aquamarine dress, matching hat, and the obligatory handbag hooked over her left arm. You catch what you're convinced is a glancing smile in your direction before she climbs into the Rolls Royce and the convoy moves off.*

*As the cavalcade leaves the palace grounds, crowds of tourists turn with cameras at the ready. Foot duty police officers hold them back as you exit the palace gates and approach the public road. Once again you become mindful of the task ahead. The ride is at speed, sometimes taking the oncoming side of the road, occasionally entering against red lights to gain control. At all times you remain calm and in control. As you and your teammates leapfrog ahead, HMQ's vehicle travels at a gentle and constant speed – never stopping unless it's completely unavoidable, or because there are simply more junctions than frogs! The royal car is easily recognizable so you can expect members of the public to try to catch a glance, wave and even try for a photo as she passes by.*

*Gaining momentum, the convoy has avoided red lights and has so far progressed with minimal disruption to the public. A few minutes away from Buckingham Palace you receive word that you are to escort Her Majesty to Windsor Castle – a routine run for the group. Despite the familiarity of the journey, none of your colleagues is in any way complacent. Indeed, the exact route is neither discussed nor decided in advance. Keeping the route open allows the officers to react to changing traffic conditions, intelligence updates and so on. You are reminded once again by something your skipper (police sergeant) said when you first arrived in the group: 'The unpredictability of the route makes it extremely difficult for an adversary to plan an attack.' You gain confidence in this wisdom.*

*Another message comes in through your headset radio but this time from your colleagues high above in the police helicopter. Although they are unaware of your exact route, or indeed destination, the air support unit has been called to what appears to be an armed robbery in progress at a bank very close to Windsor Castle. A sharp-eyed co-pilot has noticed the royal convoy from above whilst flying over Green Park. A decision is quickly made to continue but with regular updates as the robbery could result in increased security, an alternative route, a delayed arrival or even a change in the final drop off point. Although it's unlikely, you can't help but wonder if the armed men reported close to the castle are perhaps planning to attack HMQ. This is possibly more excitement than you were hoping for on your first royal run. However, you're quietly confident that your experience, training and the help of your teammates will enable you to overcome whatever challenges may lie ahead.*

*Now, twenty minutes into the run, you once again ride ahead of the convoy to the next feature. As you pass the royal car you momentarily release the throttle and glide, reducing the engine noise from your motorcycle and therefore lowering the chance of disturbing the Queen.*

*Approximately 500 metres ahead, the traffic lights at the junction you are about to control have just turned green. By the time you reach them they will have likely turned red, so you will need to stop the traffic moving left and right across the junction. A London bus packed with passengers, three saloon cars and a filthy flatbed lorry are on the road before you. Each will need to be controlled so the convoy can overtake and pass safely. As you overtake the vehicles you look through the windscreens and into the drivers' eyes to see if they are aware of your high-profile escort. A few heartbeats later you hear a series of whistle blasts as teammates to your rear begin to direct the vehicles to move over and slow down.*

*Gaining control of the junction was easy and all traffic is now stopped. A quick look in the wing mirror of your bike tells you that the convoy is about twenty seconds away. On this occasion, you decide the best way to manipulate the traffic is to dismount and direct it on foot. Standing a few metres away from your bike, which is now blocking one lane of traffic, you plant yourself in the middle of the crossroads. This gives you excellent visibility of the surrounding area. A London cabby winds down his window and shouts at you to ask 'who's coming mate?' Assessing that this was clearly an opportunistic meeting and there is no risk in telling him, you shout back: 'A royal, get your camera ready!' The cabby gives you a thumbs up and explains chirpily to his fare why they've been delayed. It's at this exact moment that you notice a child's BMX bike leaning up against a newspaper shop window.*

*The exit of the shop is directly adjacent to an empty pedestrian crossing, no more than a few metres away from where you stand. A quick glance back and you see that the convoy is now ten seconds from passing you and approaching at a steady speed. You look back to the newspaper shop and sure enough a teenage boy, wearing in-ear headphones, bopping away to his music and clutching a big bag of sweets, jumps on his bike and pushes off. Wobbling towards the pedestrian crossing, it's clear he hasn't seen the oncoming vehicles so you shout at him to stop, but he can't hear you. A firm blast of your whistle also fails to catch his attention. You freeze. Moving from your position could confuse the drivers of the stopped vehicles and risk them pulling out in front of the royal convoy. Time slows down: in fact it nearly stops as you think through what to do next.*

*Between a few more increasingly enthusiastic whistle blasts you grasp the radio and alert your fellow escorts to the incoming obstacle. If they don't see him in time, a serious accident could occur and there are only a few seconds left. Trusty Eugenie, your only female teammate, also a first timer on a royal run, acknowledges the radio alert immediately with a short, simple 'on it' response. Later that afternoon you find out that she had already seen the boy as he got on his BMX. Having also assessed the situation as dangerous, and identifying that you were unable to catch the boy's attention, she decided to rapidly increase speed and move ahead of the convoy, manoeuvring to act as a road block to the young cyclist. The consequence was that he'd come to an abrupt stop, hitting the side of her motorcycle and toppling over his handlebars before landing on her lap. This all happened just a few seconds before the convoy passed through the junction. Although it left the boy with a bruised ego and a nasty tyre mark on an immaculately-clean BMW, the tactic had worked perfectly.*

*Sitting down for a well-deserved cup of tea and handful of biscuits back in the lounge at SEG HQ, you and your teammates talk through the day's escort minute by minute, turn by turn, junction by junction, searching for ways to make improvements. You understand that this process of reflection, conducted immediately after an escort, is an important habit, which the founders of the group established back in the 1950s. The discussion takes place between the jokes and harmless mickey-taking of your panicked radio voice during the BMX incident. However, behind the banter several serious questions and ideas are raised to help improve future escorts. All mistakes are discussed openly and positively. Each officer in the SEG knows that at some stage they will make a mistake. What matters most is whether you're capable of sharing them so everyone can learn from them.*

*Your inspector leads the conversation and starts off by saying how glad he was that the armed robbery turned out to be a false alarm, but it's something worth thinking through as a scenario for future runs. All eyes turn to Eugenie as she enters the room and takes a bow in response to an unprompted round of applause. She gives you a wink and a smile. Pinning a photo of herself on the 'memories' wall, she stands back and looks at all the other pictures there. Each photograph marks a special moment during an escort – whether it is a near miss, funny incident, or something more serious. In the photo she's in full uniform, standing by her motorcycle with one leg up in the air as a playful gesture of celebration.*

*You pop another digestive biscuit in your mouth and take a sip of tea. Looking around the room at your teammates you take a step back from the discussion for a brief moment. A sense of incredible belonging and camaraderie washes over you and a vivid thought comes to mind – it's people like this, thinking like this and teamwork like this, that puts the special into the Special Escort Group.*

# The 1950s

## The Visit of Marshal Tito

The SEG, as it has been known since it began, was formed in the cold, grey, wet month of November 1952. The need to draw together a police escort was in response to a Whitehall request for enhanced security measures during the forthcoming visit of Yugoslav Prime Minister Marshal Tito in March the following year. Following on from successful post-war talks, Tito had been invited to the United Kingdom by Foreign Secretary Anthony Eden[1] during a diplomatic visit to Belgrade in September 1952.[2]

The Cold War was half a decade into maturity and political tension between the West and the Soviet Union was growing eagerly. The newly-formed Federal People's Republic of Yugoslavia had become a geo-political crossroads between the democratic West and the communist East. Tito, who was born Josip Broz, had successfully navigated his region, Yugoslavia, into a position which sat on both sides of the fence. A desirable strategic partner for the West, Tito's visit was of pronounced importance to the British Government. If relations with Tito were enhanced they would be a significant step towards strengthening the West's position against the Soviet Union.

This was to be the first time Marshal Tito had visited a western country since the creation of communist Yugoslavia in 1945. For the people of Yugoslavia, who were more culturally aligned to Russia, the visit was an important, if mostly symbolic, step towards growing closer to the modern, democratic and economically vibrant Europe. Furthermore, Tito had

---

1. Later to become prime minister (Conservative) between 1955 and 1957.
2. John Young, *Talking to Tito: the Eden Visit to Yugoslavia, September 1952* pp.31–41.

recently declared political independence from the Soviet Union and was now taking steps to build his country's economic security – a significant part of which was to be delivered through UK aid.

It was both an honour and a great responsibility for the officers from the Metropolitan Police to plan and deliver Tito's security. To the British public Tito was something of a celebrity. A former Soviet spy, he had been portrayed as a courageous military commander turned revolutionary politician and now friend of the West, so, unsurprisingly, public interest in his visit was high. Scores of crowds were expected to line the streets to witness the man in the full light of day.

Although Tito was to receive the ceremonial treatment of a head of state, it was decided that his visit would not take the full form of an official state visit.[3] Thus, protocol dictated that he would not be escorted by the cavalry on arrival in London as was traditional for visiting heads of state. Instead, an alternative but suitably ceremonial solution was required.

The security situation in London and indeed throughout the UK had, by all accounts, been relatively calm since the end of the war. Following an aggressive wave of IRA bombings across London in 1939, the last attack was in February 1940. However, there was a more specific threat against Tito. The Churchill government had been informed by their closest security and intelligence advisers, both in the UK and overseas, that Tito's visit was likely to raise public unrest. The schedule had Tito travelling between numerous high and low profile locations in and around London. His movements needed to be meticulously planned and then executed as discreetly as possible. The exact schedule for his visit was kept secret and held on a tight 'need-to-know' basis. Even Tito's departure from Yugoslavia, as well as his method of transportation to the United Kingdom, remained secret until he had almost arrived on British land.

Fearing an assassination attempt, Tito had indicated concern for his own security and had requested that appropriate security measures be taken (whilst he was beyond the protection of the Yugoslav secret police).[4] Security officials had determined that an attack was likely. Furthermore, the threat to his life

---

3. There were no state visits prior to the coronation of Her Majesty Queen Elizabeth II in 1953.
4. National Archives 371/102180.

was thought to come from such a wide range of different extremist groups and individuals that identifying them was going to be challenging. Tito needed to be surrounded by a thick, protective bubble but the question was, how would this be achieved? Following the Second World War, the Metropolitan Police suffered a significant shortfall[5] in staff so ideas that offered resource-efficient solutions were very much in fashion. It wasn't long before someone had the idea of using motorcycle escorts. The exact origin of the idea remains unsubstantiated but it is founded in the following conditions.

During the two world wars, motorcycle despatch riders from the Royal Signal Corps had been used to deliver confidential, operationally sensitive and urgent messages. An excellent tool for getting reconnaissance officers into hard to reach locations, motorcycles had proved to be superb at navigating difficult terrain without leaving much trace of their presence. They had also been essential for escorting senior military officers, as well as other VIPs, in and out of dangerous areas at speed. Back at home in the UK, military motorcycle escorts had already been used during a small number of ceremonial events outside of London. The escorts were conducted by officers of the Royal Signals' White Helmets and replaced the cavalry when it was considered too expensive or too hazardous to transport the cherished horses around the country.

The first traffic police unit, which began in 1722 at the instruction of the Lord Mayor of London, had been using motorcycles since about 1910. With the introduction of the 1930 Road Traffic Act, mobile traffic units were formed and motorbikes became a popular choice for patrolling the streets. Occasionally used to escort unusual or dangerous loads, the very first police motorcycle escorts were effective and efficient tools. It didn't take long before the newly-appointed mobile traffic officers, known to the public as the 'speed cops' formed a circus-style motorcycle display team, where they dressed up in outrageous clothing and showed off their riding skills to entertain the public. Perhaps one of their greatest shows was held in the summer of 1938 at Hendon Police College. With officers dressed in all sorts of ridiculous attire, one sorry bike, disguised as a horse, had been adjusted

---

5. Metropolitan Police Archives, 16,000 personnel with a shortfall of 4,000 police officers in 1954.

so when driven its suspension bounced its rider along. Sadly, despite their popularity, the comical display team were terminated at the outbreak of war a year later.

The first police motorcycle escorts of important individuals took place during the Festival of Britain in 1951 when they were employed to move guests and participants between the festival locations and their hotels. Without any specialist training or equipment, these trips were organized on an ad hoc basis, using officers who would normally be on traffic duties, and who were already familiar with accompanying heavy load vehicles through central London congestion.

Prior to the formation of the SEG, individuals requiring enhanced security, such as the prime minister, were provided with what is known in policing circles as 'close protection' by the Metropolitan Police's Special Branch. An armed bodyguard, or more accurately the personal protection officer (PPO) from Special Branch, was appointed to all high-risk principals (individuals who are deemed to be at significant risk of an attack against their life). The PPO would remain with the principal for the majority of their waking hours and would be on the highest alert when the principal was required to move between locations in view of the public. Usually travelling in an unmarked armoured police car, the PPO would dictate the route to the chauffeur from the front passenger seat. The principal would normally sit in the rear of the vehicle, which offered space and comfort and would often use the journey time to read official papers in preparation for their next meeting. On a normal day, the anonymous vehicle would travel solo. However, if the principal was required to participate in a public event where large crowds could be expected, additional Special Branch vehicles were added to the convoy, and the route would normally be lined with foot patrol police officers to provide additional security. This method was cumbersome, resource-intensive and expensive.

The police motorcycle escort offered an efficient and safe mode of transit between locations so it would have seemed an appropriate option for Tito's visit. It was understood by all involved in organizing the historic event that every moment would take place before the eyes of not only the British public, but by many overseas. Through the lens of the international media, even the smallest aspect of Tito's movements would be quickly and widely reported.

The newly-appointed police motorbike escort needed to be immaculately presented and move with the precision, timing, elegance and perfected degree of pomp and ceremony that had been demonstrated for decades by the much respected and admired Household Cavalry.

> 'The 1952 personnel were specifically selected for their motorcycle riding ability, temperament, smart appearance and general adaptability'. – diary notes from a retired SEG officer.

If you desire a trustworthy, diligent and inspiring team, you must appoint a trusted, proven and visionary leader. Under the direction of Inspector Arthur 'Tizzy' Tisdall, well known for his immaculately turned out uniform, a core group of twenty-two police officers were selected for the job. The men were quickly drawn into a vigorous rehearsal schedule at Hendon Police College, which would put both their individual and team-working skills to the test. The group's first members were a mixed group of personalities but they were all respected, trustworthy and well-presented officers. Senior in age and experience, most of them had a good deal of hours under their saddle riding motorcycles, but this particular event was going to challenge their skill in precision riding unlike any other before.

In his day-to-day duties Inspector Tisdall was responsible for the motorcycle training wing at the college. His regular charge was to train officers in routine traffic duties and standard vehicle roadcraft. Weeks into practice, it was decided that the parade ground and internal roads of the police college provided inadequate and unrealistic training conditions, so a nearby RAF base was commandeered temporarily. Following the notion that if you want to climb a hill, you should practise by climbing a mountain, a new and more challenging landscape was needed. Ideally, training would have taken place in a 'live' environment surrounded by the steady flow and bustle of London's traffic. However, the need to remain secretive about Tito's security preparations meant the group was denied such an opportunity. At least the open space of the airfield was beyond the prying eyes of new cadets and instructors as well as the unwelcome interference from senior officers based at the police college.

'The group were fortunate to have facilities at an RAF Station. Primarily formed for protection duties, various formations were used whilst moving, setting down, and picking up' – diary entry of a retired SEG officer.

Then there was the question of which motorcycles to select, although in those days there was really little competition. In the early 1950s, the largest and most successful producer of motorbikes in the world was Triumph (owned by the BSA – Birmingham Small Arms – Group) and as it was the preferred brand of the Metropolitan Police it was an obvious choice for the newly-formed SEG. Heavy London vehicle and pedestrian traffic generates lots of noise and this, combined with a growling pack of 500cc Triumph Speed Twin 5T motorcycle engines, meant that signalling by hand was the only way for the riders to communicate effectively. Mounted police radios, as used on conventional traffic bikes, were deemed unsightly for such a high-profile event, and in any case, they could only be used safely whilst in a stationary position. The Triumph motorcycles were low seated, upright, and relatively lightweight for their day, making them nimble and easy to handle at low speeds. They were also stunning to look at. The bodywork was finished in a rich amaranth red, and the handlebars, wheels, engine and exhaust were in polished steel and high-quality chrome. Caught in the right light, the bikes looked incredible. Manoeuvres, both slow and fast, were tried, tested and practised repeatedly until each of the officers operated faultlessly as a team. As training came to an end, partial dress rehearsals began but soon the time for practice was over.

Following a journey stretching several thousand nautical miles, Tito arrived in London aboard the naval vessel *Galeb* (Seagull) on 15 March 1953, a full day ahead of schedule. To avoid undue attention, no announcements of Tito's arrival were made public. *Galeb* was furtively anchored overnight in the Thames estuary and placed under the security of the Royal Navy. The following morning London awoke to a heavy fog, which slowed the continuation of *Galeb*'s journey up the Thames and into central London. The ship was too large to be moored at Westminster, so under careful supervision of the authorities, she was anchored close to London Bridge. Tito made the final leg of the journey to Westminster Pier onboard a small London Port Authority cruiser. Aside from the greeting party, the pier had been closed off to all but a few vetted individuals, many of whom were there to provide security.

As Tito disembarked, he was greeted by the Duke of Edinburgh, Prime Minister Winston Churchill and Foreign Secretary Anthony Eden. Although often flamboyantly robed, on this day Tito's choice of clothing was understated and he wore a simple blue military uniform, long woollen overcoat and a peaked service cap. After a series of short introductions with various heads of government service, Marshal Tito gave the following speech: 'I wish to assure the peoples [*sic*] of Great Britain that they should consider the people of my country as their staunch allies because the people of the new Yugoslavia are striving towards the same ends as the people of Great Britain.' Climbing a short flight of stone steps and walking boldly on to Victoria Embankment, Tito, together with the Duke of Edinburgh, proceeded to conduct an inspection of an honour guard comprising members of the Royal Navy.

Shortly after, Marshal Tito was shown to his vehicle. Driven by a bodyguard from the Metropolitan Police's elite Special Branch, he walked towards a shiny, black, armoured Pullman Limousine. As he approached the car, a magnesium flare thrown from the crowd set off a plume of smoke approximately forty yards away. The event caused little harm other than to startle the onlookers and the culprit was never caught. Calmly, the SEG officers started their motorcycles and manoeuvred around Tito's car, forming a tight security perimeter, before escorting the vehicle away at speed from Westminster Pier. To ensure the route ahead would remain clear, it was lined with foot duty police officers standing side by side at the edge of the pavement.

The motorcade continued towards 10 Downing Street, where Prime Minister Churchill and Tito were to hold a private meeting. As if locked together by an invisible rod, each bike was spaced apart at perfectly equal distances, forming a motorized ring of steel around the motorcade. The formation and movement of the bikes were similar to those used by the Household Cavalry whilst escorting state visitors by horse and carriage. Indeed, many of the group's earliest formations were gleaned through observation of the cavalry's ceremonial modus operandi.

For the onlookers, the sound and sight of the bikes must have been breathtaking – shining machines with loud, growling, twin exhausts; their riders aloft, bolt upright. They had the luxury limousine surrounded. Dressed from head to toe in black starched uniforms, jodhpur trousers, gaiters, black open-faced helmets, highly-polished black leather boots and fighter pilot style goggles, they rolled on forward. One might liken the spectacle in sound, sight and atmosphere to a group of Spitfire planes escorting a Bristol Blenheim bomber.

The group escorted Tito to and from all of his appointments in and around London, of which there were many, formal and informal. The most prominent was an audience with HMQ at Buckingham Palace, followed by lunch – an honour bestowed on only a few. Although Tito's visit to the UK was not defined as an official state visit, in the eyes of the public, an audience with HMQ legitimized his importance as both a state leader and a friend of Britain. From a symbolic perspective, Tito's meeting at Buckingham Palace was the most important part of his trip.

The final leg of his British tour saw Tito return to Westminster Pier, where he'd first touched English soil. Due to the worsening weather, the SEG officers were now dressed in a standard police issue motorcycle Mackintosh. The Mackintosh had a very wide back designed to sit over the saddle of the bike, similar to the capes used by the cavalry. To stop them flapping about the 'macs' had fabric toggles inside which buttoned around the legs – seen from behind they looked like very large nappies! To keep out the wet and the cold, they wore white gauntlets on their hands, which were ideal for allowing the hand to be seen when giving signals and directing traffic. As the motorcade arrived at the pier, the officers manoeuvred around Tito's vehicle and came to rest ahead of his car, in a long arrowhead formation. Once again, and despite weather conditions, they were immaculately presented, on time and had executed the escort with total precision.

Tito's final charge was to conduct a departure inspection of the honour guard, together with the British foreign minister, before boarding the cruiser, which had brought him into Westminster Pier several days before. The visit had been a huge success for all parties involved. With no mishaps or security incidents worthy of note, the Metropolitan Police, with the SEG at the forefront, had not only done their duty but had exceeded all expectations. They had made both the government and the great British public proud. That week, the nation's newspapers were full of articles about the SEG and its role in Tito's visit. The group had laid down its first cornerstone on which to build.

While the visit of Marshal Tito would lay a foundation in western Cold War strategy, this was also to be the first historic milestone for the group. Despite impressive beginnings, SEG was to remain on a temporary footing for many years to come – only drawn together on special ceremonial occasions. In the first years, requests for the SEG were usually made by Whitehall staff and endorsed by senior officers at New Scotland Yard. The group would then be reformed and rehearsed at Hendon Police College. Months could go by between escorts, during which time those appointed to the SEG would return to normal, and often rather less exciting police duties. As one retired officer joked: 'For a time work dropped off, and we had to go out on anti-parking patrols. I believe one parking ticket was issued. We kept a photocopy of it in the office for years.'

## The Queen's Coronation

Having won the trust of Whitehall officials during Tito's visit, the group soon found itself at the forefront of the planning and execution of HMQ's coronation tour of London. The tour would see the newly-crowned Queen chauffeured and shown off across the capital for all to see. The group's specific role was to provide an escort to the royal convoy.

The tour followed two days after the coronation, which took place on 2 June 1953, and was planned by officers working from the famous Canon Row Police Station located just behind Whitehall in Westminster. A subset of New Scotland Yard, Canon Row Police Station was responsible for policing Buckingham Palace, Windsor Castle, The Palace of Westminster, 10 Downing Street, Clarence House, St James' Palace as well as all major events and demonstrations in central London.

The coronation took place at Westminster Abbey. The event drew over 8,000 invited guests and was watched on television by an estimated twenty-seven million people in Britain alone. A further eleven million listened in on the radio. Approximately 29,000 police and military personnel were appointed to support the event, yet it would be just a small number of officers from the SEG that would be watched by millions in every corner of the planet. The magnitude of the event was unprecedented and the SEG was charged with performing at the highest levels of ceremonial perfection. Days preceding the tour were spent stripping down each motorcycle for a total clean, polish and check over to ensure it would be fit for purpose on the day – a routine that remained with the group for years to come.

The royal family hoped that as many members of the public as possible would get to see the procession as close up as possible. Unlike Tito's escorts, which were conducted at a swift but steady speed, this procession was to move slowly through large crowds and this made precision riding especially important. With a motorcycle on each corner of the royal cars, and hundreds of foot patrol officers lining the route, traffic junctions were closed as the group skilfully escorted HMQ's motorcade across much of London, passing by millions of excited onlookers. One retired SEG officer recalled being a young boy and waiting at a crossroads close to his family home to see the new Queen go by:

'I was stood with my parents trying to peek a look at the road through the legs of a crowd of adults. I managed to squeeze myself to the front and was now stood at the edge of the kerb. In that second the Queen's own car appeared and stopped directly beside me. For a magical moment I was stood face to face with HMQ. Perhaps this was one of the things that inspired me to join the group years later.'

As the procession moved along, it was met with roars and cheers from the waving crowds. For the SEG officers, the sight and sound of the appreciative masses would have been an incredible, uplifting experience. The upright riding position and open-faced helmets gave the officers good visibility of the route ahead. Although the weather during most of May had been good, Coronation Day itself had suffered from a dramatic drop in temperature and, sadly, several downpours of rain. This wasn't good news for the SEG. Puddles splash and spoil uniforms. From the saddle of a motorcycle, thin layers of water on the road can be difficult to spot, making it potentially slippery and therefore risky to manoeuvre quickly. The weather added to the list of potential hazards. The possibility of someone jumping out between the sparsely-spaced foot patrol officers and disrupting the flow of the procession could also not be ruled out. Furthermore, the procession route covered so much of London that it was unrealistic to check in advance for hazardous spills or slippery litter. The group needed to demonstrate great care and focus as the smallest mistake could unsettle the whole event.

In many areas, the vast, heaving crowds had breached the pavements and stood eagerly waiting on the roads, leaving only a narrow, if occasionally swelling, canal for the escort to pass through. To assist in maintaining a clear passage, a method of advance warning was borrowed from the armed forces. A single officer would ride his motorcycle several hundred metres ahead of the motorcade displaying a picture of a red diamond.[6] The symbol would indicate to foot patrol officers waiting ahead that the procession would soon be upon them. On sight of the red diamond they would close junctions and start the difficult work of pushing back and controlling the crowds. In a similar vein, a single motorcycle would travel at the rear of the motorcade displaying a white diamond, which would indicate to foot patrol officers that the motorcade had now passed them by. The system of using red and white diamonds in this way worked extremely well and continues to be used by SEG today.

The coronation and public tour gained great public approval in the following weeks. Hundreds of thousands of people had gained a once in a lifetime opportunity of seeing the young Queen in the flesh for the first time since her accession to the throne. For a few fleeting moments one could easily be forgiven for thinking the SEG was the star of the show. Headlining in various print outlets and the subject of fulsome praise and complimentary discussion on radio, the skill and planning of the group grabbed everyone's attention. Once again, the group performed faultlessly, further proving that the stylish method of motorcycle escort was reliable, safe, elegant and efficient. Importantly, the SEG had demonstrated with striking clarity that it was capable of providing an escort befitting a monarch.

---

6. The idea of using a red diamond symbol in this way originates from the armed forces. In a military context the symbol is associated with Battalion HQ vehicles and represents a spearhead. The red diamond spearhead is also the insignia of the 1st Corps of the Army, the Royal Military Police 'flash' as well as a number of other regiments.

## The Russians are Coming

Three years on from the coronation, the spotlight was once again on the team. With cameras poised, the world's press was watching, recording and reporting everything because a goodwill visit was flavour of the day. Soviet Premier (Prime Minister) Nikolai Bulganin and First Secretary Nikita Khrushchev were to become the first Soviet leaders to visit the UK since the establishment of the Soviet Union some thirty-four years earlier.

Travelling to the UK by sea on the Soviet Navy cruiser *Ordzhonikidze*, they arrived on 18 April 1956 at Portsmouth Harbour. They were greeted by the Russian Ambassador to the UK and an honour guard from HMS *Victory*. As many as 4,000 members of the public lined the route from the harbour to the railway station where they boarded a steam train for Victoria Station. On arrival in London they were greeted by British Prime Minister Sir Anthony Eden as well as several key members of his government. Following two short televised speeches offering the usual declarations of improved relations, the Soviet leaders, together with their hosts and guests, walked outside the station to be met by a convoy of black limousines together with their SEG escort. Most of the old team, along with one or two new faces, had been rallied together by the police college for what was to be a high-security visit. The schedule was packed tight, with dozens of meetings at various locations in London and its environs. Since timing was crucial, once again pick-up points, routes and drop-off points would need to be planned and rehearsed meticulously.

Some things, however, were beyond the control of the planners. During the eight days of their visit, the Soviets were met either by silent or jeering crowds. Many waved anti-Soviet banners. With the Cold War now in full swing, the public mood was one of suspicion and disregard. Deception and mistrust had characterized relations between the West and Russia for years but during the world wars this had been tempered by an alliance against the Germans. Now they no longer shared a common enemy, a violent clash of ideologies and political visions between the authoritarian communist East and the democratic capitalist West seemed inevitable. The world was once again poised for war.

In 1949, the West had formed the NATO (North Atlantic Treaty Organization) alliance with the purpose of deterring Soviet expansionism, forbidding the revival of nationalist militarism in Europe and encouraging greater political integration across Europe. From a Soviet perspective, NATO was a clear demonstration of western force – a threat. From a western perspective, the Soviet Union had gained concerning allegiances of its own across much of Eastern Europe, as well as many of its own border countries. Worryingly for the British political elite, support for communism in the UK had increased since the end of the war. By 1945, over 97,000 people had registered as members of the Communist Party in Great Britain. The Labour Party had also seen a significant number of members shift allegiance to communist ideologies; especially union officials from across industry, particularly coal mining. In hope of inspiring the British communists, the Soviet leaders hoped their visit would trigger a communist uprising across the UK.

It's unlikely the SEG was aware of the intelligence operations that would have taken place between the shadows of the Soviets' visit. However, since the group had near complete oversight of the leaders' whereabouts while in the UK, its presence created opportunities for the British intelligence agencies to keep Bulganin and Khrushchev under a watchful eye. In an era of atom bombs, espionage, an arms and a space race, clandestine intelligence-gathering operations drove government decision-making. Intelligence was thought to be the best way for both sides to stay one step ahead of each other. The Soviets' own entourage would have certainly included a number of senior Soviet spies there to take advantage of whatever opportunities may arise. Beneath the veneer and the visible, the visit would provide both sides with important intelligence-gathering opportunities – such an occasion simply couldn't be ignored.

The UK's own intelligence agencies would have also been on full alert. For example, the cruiser *Ordzhonikidze* was placed under close observation by a Royal Navy team of secret frogman divers. Working on the reasonable assumption that Soviet spies would use the cruiser as a secure base, it was decided that there could be much to learn by monitoring her closely. Indeed, one of the frogmen, Lionel Kenneth Phillip Crabb, popularly known as 'Buster Crabb', is reported to have been deployed on behalf of MI6 to conduct underwater surveillance of the cruiser. The propeller of the vessel, a new design, was of particular interest to naval intelligence. Tragically, Crabb failed to return from his mission. The exact circumstances behind his disappearance remain a mystery but many believe he was caught and murdered by a security team onboard the ship.

The first escort was to be a relatively short run, mostly on main roads, moving the convoy from Victoria Station to the famous Claridge's Hotel – a favoured choice of many heads of state and their families while visiting London. The highly-visible route took them along Grosvenor Place, across the western edge of Green Park, into Park Lane and finally alongside Hyde Park. In contrast to the background of flowers lined up like soldiers by the royal parks' gardeners, the pavements were lined with members of the public, most with an unwelcome glare in their eyes, who were there to catch a glimpse of the controversial visitors.

Newspaper photographs illustrating articles covering the visit show that the group used what is known as a 'box formation'. Created especially for ceremonial escorts this formation was used originally by the Household Cavalry during state visits. The method is typical when the convoy is required to weave through tightly-packed crowds which might leave only a few metres of open space either side of the VIP vehicle. The layout is constructed as follows: a single motorcycle sits at each wheel of the VIP and Special Branch vehicles, four bikes ahead of the convoy form an arrowhead (red diamond in the lead), then two motorcycles form a rear guard immediately behind a marked police car. The rear guard is there primarily to prevent following traffic from overtaking the convoy. The box could be decreased in size to a 'closed box' or increased to an 'open box', with both the motorbikes and cars moving further away and closer in depending on what level of security was best at that moment. The formation not only looked impressive, it also provided each of the group with good visibility while moving through dense crowds. The formation also allowed officers the opportunity to react quickly and dynamically to threats, especially those coming from either side of the convoy.

'Training for the Russian leaders' visit was extensive, took place between March and April of 1956. SEG officers gathered over 50 hours of riding, and a total of 200 miles per machine. There were a number of new members in the group, so the training was entirely justified.' – diary entry of a retired SEG officer.

Over the remaining days of the visit, the group escorted the leaders to Buckingham Palace, Windsor Castle, St Paul's Cathedral, London Airport and Downing Street as well as to Chequers (the residence of the British Prime Minister). Whenever the convoy met the public, it received the same muted reaction. The crowds seemed entirely impervious to the temptation to cheer, but utterly enticed by the lure to jeer. Despite the prevailing peer pressure, the group remained visually neutral and professionally courteous at all times. And they were all the more respected for doing so. One retired officer, who remembered listening to stories from his older colleagues, said: 'If the crowds did cheer, it was for the ever-increasingly popular SEG and certainly not the Soviets.'

## The visit of President Eisenhower

As the months passed, the escorts became more frequent. The period spanning 1957 to 1959 was to prove particularly progressive with the group being called into action on numerous occasions. During this time, there were two historically significant milestones: a US presidential visit and the formation of the Motorcycle Precision Team.

On 27 August 1959, Dwight David Eisenhower became the third American president ever to visit the UK. He was also the first president of any country that the SEG would be charged to escort. Prior to his political career, Eisenhower had held the position as NATO's first Supreme Allied Commander. A veteran of both world wars, he was perhaps one of the most popular American generals. As president, his popularity continued to grow.

Although this was an informal visit, Eisenhower's intentions were clear. As part of an international tour, his aim was to discuss shared concerns and areas of interest about the Soviet Union, not only with Britain, but with all the leaders of the western alliance. His objective was to be fully prepared for planned talks in September later that year with First Secretary Khrushchev at the White House. This would be the first time a communist leader was to attend a meeting with the US Government on American soil.

Rehearsed, ready and now experienced in high-profile events, the SEG was fit for its next mission. Once again, the group was to employ Triumph Speed Twin 5T motorcycles. However, unlike previous escorts, which comprised a small number of cars, this one was to include numerous US Secret Service vehicles. This increased fleet of cars would stretch previously employed convoy methods to the max, so a new system and set of motorcycle formations were designed accordingly. The president's own vehicle was a stretched open-top Silver Cloud Rolls Royce.

The escort started at London City Airport where President Eisenhower was greeted by Prime Minister Harold Macmillan. The convoy then proceeded to tour across London passing by many of the city's major landmarks. It was a wonderful sight for the public as Eisenhower stood in an open-topped car, waving at the crowds from a rear footwell. However, such exposure made one of the most powerful men in the world a far more vulnerable target for an attacker than if he'd been transported in one of Special Branch's armoured vehicles. With no known specific threat against the president, his security team had judged that it was safe to allow maximum public visibility; a decision that no doubt placed significant worry on the shoulders of the SEG.

The Metropolitan Police's security team, which included the SEG, needed to work in coordination with the president's own large security team. However, due to their separate locations, there had been limited opportunity to practise in advance. Culturally the methodology of the two teams was far apart, with the British preferring a relatively low-key security posture compared to their US counterparts. Much of the security planning was done months ahead of the president's arrival in the UK. Fortunately, relations with the Secret Service's liaison team based at the American Embassy in London were strong. Nevertheless, without the possibility of a full dress rehearsal, both teams were tense at the thought of working together for the first time at such a high-profile event. Especially when it was taking place right before the eyes of the world's media.

Following his tour in London, intended mostly to please the British public, Eisenhower was then escorted to a private meeting with Prime Minister Macmillan at Chequers in Buckinghamshire. He then completed his visit by attending an audience with HMQ at her Scottish home, Balmoral Castle.

The first presidential escort was over. A team relationship between the SEG and the American Secret Service was forged and it is one that remains solid to this day. And to the merit and ingenuity of all involved, the escorts were an 'uneventful success', which is the best result an SEG officer could hope for.

## The Motorcycle Precision Team

The SEG's popularity had reached new and unpredicted heights. The British press had reported widely on the officers' skills, always placing them in a positive light. The refined display of precision, the clockwork accuracy and the immaculate presentation delighted the public and they wanted to see more. Following the escort of Eisenhower, the Metropolitan Police received a large number of letters and telephone calls from people requesting to meet with the group. After a short period of consultation between senior management and the group itself, it was announced that the Motorcycle Precision Team (MPT) would be formed in order to entertain the SEG's many fans and demonstrate the officers' skills on two wheels. However, mindful that popularity can poison the roots of success, the decision wasn't made lightly. The core team comprised SEG officers, added to by a growing number of 'strappers' (officers temporarily attached – 'strapped' – to the SEG) from across the garages of B Department (Traffic). All were eager to join in the fun. Not only did the demonstrations and rides entertain and excite, they also provided a wonderful recruitment tool for the Metropolitan Police. Crucially, they also delivered important messages about road traffic safety. The primary aim of the first public display in the summer of 1959 was to inspire fellow motorcyclists to become safer riders.

From the outset, the MPT was in high demand and quickly established a name (often called the 'Peggy Spencers' after the famous ballroom dancer) and reputation for being world–class leaders in high and low speed riding based upon safety and precision handling. Jumps, tricks and daredevil stunts were not for these police riders who, instead, aimed to showcase their ability to handle their bikes safely and teach amateurs tips, which could be used on public roads. School fetes and county shows would play host to the MPT so thousands of people could witness high speed cross overs and complex formations similar to those used during an escort. New moves were thought out on paper first and then walked through on foot. Officers would then try the manoeuvre out slowly to see if it worked well and looked good. Speed was then increased and timings were worked out visually as there were no sound prompts or hand signals. The main way of keeping everything slick was to read each motorcycle's movements or, as one officer put it: 'You'd try and clip the rear mud plate without actually doing it. The tighter the cross over the more the crowd cheered.'

Mistakes did happen but thankfully, they took place during practice and dress rehearsals. 'One eager rookie to the team lasted only fifteen minutes before crashing into the rear of another motorcycle, and then deciding it wasn't for him,' explained one officer. On another occasion, a new rider was dismounted by a surprise patch of wet grass. As he lay on the floor with a broken wrist, all he could say was he would 'miss the doughnut', which was the traditional after-ride treat. 'This self-critical appraisal,' continued the officer, 'often aided by a mate shouting in your ear, gave officers an informal system of reviewing performance and developing new ideas.' The system of review was to eventually become a permanent feature of the SEG's work ethic, embedded deep into the group's DNA.

Running alongside the SEG for close to forty years, the MPT played an important role in the continued refinement of escort routines and formations. Practice sessions for displays allowed members to test out and tinker with new techniques, while improving their motorcycling skills, and of course developing communication further. New machines, updated radio kit, better uniforms and much more were tested. As one retired officer said: 'Morale and the feeling of team spirit was high in the SEG, but it was even higher in the precision team.' SEG officers who were not members of the MPT learnt from the ideas, techniques and advice that came out of hours and hours of laborious practice. Indeed, as one proud MPT member said cheekily: 'It has always been a joke that members of the precision team would describe themselves as the precision team on which the SEG is based.'

**Triumph Speed Twin 5T (1952–1959 approx).** Originally designed in 1937, the 500cc Speed Twin was a sporty and nimble motorcycle for its time. Popular with both civilians and the police, the SEG selected the distinct amaranth red body paint and, combined with gleaming chrome and polished steel metalwork, the bike was a spectacular sight. Minor alterations were made for its use with the SEG. The motorcycle was first brought into service with the SEG for the visit of Marshal Tito in 1953. Tito himself is said to have commented on the elegant look of the motorcycle. In 1978, twenty-five years after his first visit to the UK and two years before his death, Tito made a final visit to London. Once again, the SEG was employed to escort him. At the conclusion of his visit, the SEG returned him to the steps of his aircraft, where he was presented with a photo of the men and motorcycles that had escorted him back in 1953. Tito is said to have been rather touched by the gesture.

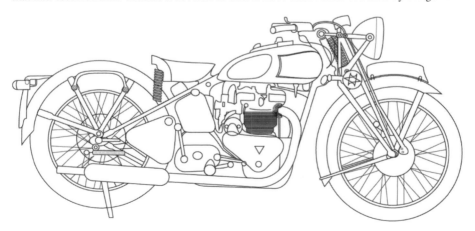

# The 1960s

## Changes in Leadership

The beat of London's streets is said to have become fabulously free spirited. With the arrival of the 'Mods' and the 'Rockers', motorcycles had become the must-have accessory for all those born to be wild. The fashionable young hipsters of London were no exception and two-wheeled transport ruled the roads. For attention-seeking car lovers, Austins painted with psychedelic swirls and abstract art were the preferred uptown runabout. But there was little that was wild or far out about the SEG. With the soberly-dressed officers riding impressively turned out machines protecting those who represented the aristocracy or the establishment, SEG struck a note with the British public more attuned to Beethoven than the Beatles.

The 1960s was renowned for espousing peace and love and there weren't any specific threats targeting high-profile persons in the UK during that time. With an extended agenda of non-violent action from the IRA (Irish Republican Army), the threat from terrorism seemed negligible. However, the security community understood that those who wish to do harm will often attempt to charm and deceive us and complacency is never an option. As is too often true in the field of national security, absence of evidence is rarely evidence of absence. On this basis, SEG protective security measures continued to grow.

As the SEG's list of completed escorts grew longer, so did the team's appreciation for the security threats posed to the VIPs in its charge. Overseas, several high-profile officials had been assassinated while under the care of foreign protection teams. Perhaps the most notable of these was President John F. Kennedy in 1963. While horrified by the tragic circumstances surrounding these events, the British security community, including the SEG, also learnt what it could from such incidents.

The greatest assessed threat was believed to be from a rogue individual's intent on achieving notoriety and making a name for themselves. This was closely followed by kidnap for financial or political gain. Unarmed, there was little the SEG could do to fight back in the event of a serious or well-organized attack. In this event, the group would have to rely on the combined experience of its officers gleaned from decades of policing London. Everything was aimed at protection, and training had been focused solely on shielding the escort's dignity and moving them to safety. The VIP vehicle contained at least one armed Special Branch officer and in the event of an armed ambush, that officer would attempt to fend off the offenders single-handedly. Despite this obvious vulnerability little would be done to address this until the 1970s.

In what was fast becoming known as one of the roughest parts of London, the East End had become home to numerous organized-crime syndicates who'd built their lucrative, illegal empires by exploiting post-war economic growth. The dreary and damp Thames Docks provided links to more exotic locations in far reaching corners of the world. Traditional cockney, grey market trading was morphing into a darker more sinister shade. An increase in maritime traffic generated legitimate cover for illegal operations, and the sprawling chaos of the bustling but dilapidated dockyards provided excellent opportunities for organized smugglers to network and safely store their commodities. A growing demand for recreational drugs generated huge profits, making many of the criminals powerful, dangerous and influential. Some of them were known to carry firearms, and as competition against their interests grew, so did a willingness to use violence.

As police cracked down on the criminal gangs, a great number of arrests were made. A specialist team of police officers, known as Special Patrol Group (SPG), was responsible for the movement of these prisoners, many of whom were considered to be extremely dangerous. The SPG used secure vans and marked police cars to move the offenders. Occasionally traffic duty police motorcyclists were used to escort the prison vans. From the perspective of even the most careful observer, an SPG escort could easily be confused with an SEG escort. Thus, the possibility of a hardened criminal gang attempting to recover one of its own using force and firearms during an SEG escort could never be ruled out.

Conscious of the growth of an increasingly complex range of escorts, a new era of security preparedness lay ahead for the SEG. With these changes came new training, new equipment and a host of new protection methods.

At the turn of the decade, almost eight years had passed since the founding days at Hendon. After retiring with distinction in 1957, Inspector Arthur Tisdall was awarded the British Empire Medal for his role in forming the SEG. His departure triggered a discussion about where the growing group should be homed. The diary of future escorts was getting full, and the MPT was in increasingly high demand. Time had come for the group to receive a more permanent position within the police structure and the decision was made for it to move away from the management at Hendon Police College and join the traffic police division.

In 1959, Charles Jean Day, or 'Dicky' to his officers, was appointed as the replacement to Inspector Tisdall. Day, born in 1913, was a country lad from the south west of England and the youngest of eleven siblings. Seeking out the excitement of London, he joined the Metropolitan Police in 1934. During the war years, he served in the Royal Navy aboard minesweeper HMS *Havelock*, rejoining the Metropolitan Police at the end of the conflict. 'My dad was a popular man with his officers and a diligent and dedicated officer,' said his daughter Anne McCarthy. Indeed, his dedication to SEG saw him turn down an opportunity to become Princess Margaret's bodyguard, preferring to stay with his team. 'Dad remained with the group until a year prior to his retirement,' explained Anne. During this time, he met with many world leaders and VIPs including President Kennedy, Russian cosmonaut Yuri Gagarin, Queen Frederica of Greece, and Prime Minister Macmillan. Anne revealed that Macmillan had personally thanked her father for his work with the SEG. 'I remember Dad saying that the prime minister had a very firm handshake,' she added with a laugh.

In addition to his role with the SEG, Inspector Day remained a full-time supervisor for several hundred regular traffic officers, so it wasn't long before he found himself with fewer hours than he had tasks. In 1960, after just a few months of arriving at SEG, Inspector Day appointed his second in command, Sergeant John Baldwin, to take over as head of the MPT and shoulder responsibility for leading the daily operations of the SEG. The MPT had been extremely popular with the public and the rising demand for displays commanded careful management. Sergeant Baldwin, a veteran of the Second World War, had begun his career with the Royal Engineers, leaving to join the Metropolitan Police in 1947. With a keen interest in motorcycles, he had joined the traffic division, which is also where he first met the SEG.

Inspector Day retired in 1963 and Baldwin, who was already de facto head of the SEG, was his obvious replacement. Young, enthusiastic, and extremely popular with the rest of the group, he was soon promoted to inspector, taking over full responsibility of the SEG's operations. Not only was he the first permanent head of the group; he was also to become one of the longest serving of all time. While with the SEG, he rose from sergeant to superintendent in thirteen years, a feat achieved by few in the history of the Metropolitan Police. His career achievements are an acknowledgment of his professionalism, dedication, vision, leadership and contribution to the continued refinement of the SEG. His influence on the group cannot be underestimated, as Colin Tebbutt MVO (Member of the Royal Victorian Order) explained: 'John Baldwin was a true professional in the world of police protection and VIP escorts. His hard work in his preparation and delivery became a lead for the future of the SEG. He cemented a formula of escorts with motorcycles and cars that has been admired, and copied, the world over.'

I had the privilege of meeting with John Baldwin and his wife at their family home in a leafy suburb of south-east London. It was a hot, sunny day and I was running a little late – thank you public transport. As I checked my watch, I worried about what he'd think of me arriving late. After all, this was a man who had spent much of his career stepping to the tick of a clock. I asked myself whether HMQ would have forgiven John if he'd arrived at Buckingham Palace late.

Standing outside a large and well-presented 1940s house, I rang the bell. After being greeted by his wife Joyce, I was politely ushered in and directed towards the living room. There I found John sat quietly in his armchair surrounded by books and photographs. Lifting his hand and casually pointing at the floor, he said 'don't mind the dog, he's a bit old and deaf, but he's OK. Now come in and sit down and tell me about your project.' John was soon to celebrate his 90th birthday.

At his invitation, I sat down on a comfortable sofa and looked at the tall and once athletic man before me. He was welcoming but serious. I liked him immediately. Calm, cool and collected, he had an air of confidence and wisdom earned from an advanced course at the university of life. An English gentleman to the definition, he had fought and survived a war, shaken the hands of presidents, conversed with emperors and sipped tea with the first man and woman in space. Yet despite his many professional achievements he was first and foremost a family man whose greatest accomplishments were being a husband, father and grandfather.

As he began to ask me questions, I couldn't help but notice the way in which he sat in his chair. His posture was very similar to the way he sat on a motorcycle in many of the pictures I studied prior to our meeting. It was as if his body had been moulded that way after so many years in the saddle.

After a couple of minutes of locating mutual connections and a discussion about my dad, David Jagger, whom he'd met some years before, I asked him about his life in the SEG. 'I took over the unit as a going concern,' he said. 'At first I was attached to the Motorcycle Precision Team, taking over from another sergeant, but I was soon working together with the SEG.' I asked him about the motorbikes: 'We used Triumph motorcycles. Great bikes, reliable, not very powerful, which didn't really matter, but they did leak a lot of oil, so they were a bit of a pain to keep clean.'

Before I could ask any further questions, Joyce came into the living room with a tray of teas and biscuits, asking 'is John being well behaved?' Seeing the cups, John asked if I'd prefer a beer. His wife looked at me, winked, shook her head and smiled as she walked back to the kitchen. This was just the sort of cheerful cheekiness I'd come to expect, having heard so many stories from those who'd served with him. Whilst pouring milk into our cups, I took a moment to glance around the living room. Not a single sign of his career could be seen. There wasn't a picture on the walls, shelves or the mantelpieces. How unusual, I thought, as my eyes searched a little further.

As we chatted, it became increasingly clear how influential John had been on the culture and personality of the SEG. Sharp-witted, good-humoured, level-headed, diplomatic and politically astute, I could see why he had made such an exceptional leader. Admired by his team, and trusted and respected by his superiors, his reputation within SEG and royalty protection circles is legendary.

He regaled me with many happy memories, all delivered with enthusiasm and pride. I decided to turn the conversation on its head and ask him what was his least favourite escort. 'It was the Russians leaders,' he said without hesitation. 'Their security liaison officers refused to cooperate with us in any way. They didn't seem to understand the need-to-know rule. They kept things that shouldn't be secret, secret and they had a habit of interfering in our route plans at the last minute.' Usually the SEG would be in total control of the route and the timings of an escort.

'We collected the two Russian leaders,' he said. 'Mr Kosygin, and Mr Brezhnev, together with their advisers, and their own security team, from Claridge's Hotel on Brook Street in Mayfair. Our destination was Whitehall. Our route would have us travel away from the hotel, along Grosvenor Square and then left into Park Lane, before proceeding into Westminster.' John smiled, sat back in his chair and continued:

'As we drove along Park Lane, with Hyde Park on our right-hand side, the Russian leaders' limousine came to a sudden stop. This was very much unexpected. Before we had a chance to speak to the driver, both of the Russians had leapt out of the vehicle and were jogging towards the park. Not quite out of sight, we could see them both meet with a couple of men in dark clothing. They stood close to a park bench and spoke to each other for several minutes before returning to the motorcade.'

Despite this breach of protocol, which apparently happened several times during their visit, John said he and his colleagues 'ploughed on stumbling along as best as we could. These were incredibly sensitive times. If something had happened to them it could have started World War Three.'

He stressed the importance of teamwork in SEG and of not taking each other too seriously, even if the job demanded seriousness at all times. 'The chaps met challenges head on and always got the job done,' said John. 'I had total trust in them and never regretted hiring a single one. We kept sharp because we encouraged self-criticism. In fact I insisted on it. We worked hard, we were immaculate, precise, disciplined, but always kept a playful spirit whilst on the job.' I've spoken to dozens of retired and current SEG officers who served across decades of the group's history and they all say this attitude remains in SEG to this day. This is John's legacy.

Many of the officers who'd been appointed to escort Tito were of retirement age by the time John Baldwin took over. Loaded with energy and with a bright vision for the SEG, John was in a position to hire new officers. 'Continuity in the team was extremely important,' he said. 'Striking a balance of old timers and newcomers, meant that high standards were maintained, new ideas were encouraged, and escorting techniques were constantly improved.' Officers were selected on the basis of their reputation and their track record. Most of the time they were recommended to John by other supervisors, usually from within the traffic police community. John, quite correctly, was only interested in individuals that could demonstrate the highest possible standards in their work. In fact, they needed to excel.

Although he worked with too many exceptional individuals to name, John shared memories of many of his officers including Don Gibbons, Ron Hales, John Wilding and Ray Young, who was the youngest of all John's recruits, joining the MPT aged just 26. 'My right-hand man was a fellow called Jock Shields,' said John. 'One of the more experienced in the team; a disciplined man, a firm but friendly Scotsman, well respected by the troops, and a reliable pair of hands. He always knew how to get the job done and I relied on him often.'

A man of many talents, one of Sergeant Jock Shields' greatest contributions to the group was to lock in routines and rituals that kept the team disciplined and dedicated to precision. He achieved this by developing a collection of handbooks that set the foundations for the SEG's complex tradecraft. Taking over from John as head of the MPT, Jock served with the SEG as deputy leader between 1966 and 1976, during which time he became one of the best known officers in the Metropolitan Police. Often stepping up into John's shoes as the lead officer in escorts, Sergeant Shields also took the MPT to hundreds of shows across the country during his tenure. As deputy leader, he assumed the responsibility for the overall smartness and discipline of the group.

'Jock will be remembered as an accomplished rider, always of immaculate turn-out, who led from the front setting excellent standards for his team. With his great sense of humour and loyalty to his colleagues he was a popular figure with everyone who worked with him. He was proud of the role played by the SEG and the Display Team and conscious that on many occasions the reputation of the force was being judged by the way that they performed their duty and the impressions that were left behind. The wide respect held today for the SEG reflects the successful influence of Jock and his colleagues in laying the foundations and traditions of the present day group.' Jock Shields' obituary in Clearway Magazine.

Occasionally friends and family would attend the MPT's public displays to cheer on the team, and admire and take pride in the skill of their loved ones. There were also private displays for the police community, usually at the Warren Social Club in Bromley, Kent. Jock's daughter, Diane Davis, remembered being 7-years-old when 'the guys would put a child in the front, and another behind them on the bikes, then set off briskly around the field. No helmets were worn! Since I was the daughter of the skipper I could jump the queue.'

As he continued to speak about his former colleagues, John graciously gave them much of the credit for helping set the group's high standards. With a great deal of pride in his voice, and sitting a little more upright and pronounced, he said: 'I hired Colin Tebbutt, a great man and an exceptional member of the team. Even then it was clear he'd go on to great things.'

A little over twelve years John's junior, Colin had started his career as a Royal Marine commando prior to joining the police. Hugely respected by his colleagues, he was known to be charismatic, quick-witted, charming and always immaculately turned out. John had first sized Colin up during the investiture ceremony of the Prince of Wales in 1969. By the end of the event, John had offered Colin a position in the group and he would go on to serve the SEG twice with intervals during which he worked in other specialist police departments. On promotion and a consequent departure from the SEG, Colin became a personal protection officer to numerous members of the royal family, including HRH Princess Anne. He was eventually honoured with the MVO for his service. Whatever John had seen in Colin proved correct. During Colin's tenure with the SEG, he was instrumental in developing the group, gracefully crafting the methods to take an increasingly hostile security environment into account. His efforts included introducing the first firearms to the SEG. He also focused on networking so the group became better known in other police departments and within the government, which helped the SEG gain regular and high-quality work. Having established a unique trust with several members of the royal family, he played an influential, if not primary, part in solidifying the group's role of providing them with regular escorts.

Another person for whom John had nothing but respect was Police Constable (PC) Trevor Pryke, a man who I was fortunate enough to interview.

An innovator at heart, John said: 'Trevor was always at the forefront of whatever we were doing, always cheerful and a leading light for the others to follow.' Trevor did indeed whistle while he worked. In fact he introduced the whistle to SEG escorts, as well as co-founding the motto 'We Lead Others Follow' – two stories that will be detailed later in this book.

Trevor had joined the Met Police Cadet Force as recruit number 461:

'During my cadet service I was posted to Wembley Traffic Patrol Garage, known as DT2 internally to the police. Here I met with two officers of the Special Escort Group – PC Ron Jamieson and PC Reg Leah (both now deceased). I made it part of my attachment to look after their bikes. In truth, this is where I learnt about the SEG. From this moment on it became my goal to become a member.'

Trevor became a PC at 19 and was posted to Marylebone Lane D Division. 'I remained there for two years and when I was 23 I applied for Traffic Patrol and was accepted and posted to Wembley Garage. I was the youngest member of Traffic Patrol at that time in the Met.' On 10 September 1963 he was accepted into the SEG. It was, he said 'the proudest moment of my career'.

'The SEG was held in great esteem and received a lot of coverage by the newsreels at the time,' explained Trevor. 'It was regarded as the most professional and prestigious police escort group in the world.' All heads of states were happy to be escorted by the group.

Trevor, and his close teammate Bob Caswell (of whom more later) were to become an important influence on the continued evolution of the SEG's working practices. Some of their ideas were ingenious and still play a crucial role today in the successful execution of police motorcycle escorts.

Having brought new blood into the team, it was now time for Sergeant John Baldwin to elevate the training regime, to take into account an increasingly large workload and the range of escorts now required.

The group's training events during the 1950s and 1960s were engineered primarily to achieve high levels of presentation, safety and timing. Indeed, even in today's security environment these three elements remain key. The basic training for police vehicle handling was founded on the principles of Lord Cottenham's 'Roadcraft' which coined the phrase: 'Right place, right time, right speed, right gear.' Delivering the passenger to their destination on time in a manner befitting their status was the chief focus. Security was unquestionably an important feature of any run. Yet in the absence of specialist security training, officers had little more than faith in the experience they'd gained as weather-hardened London bobbies to keep them upright in the event of an incident.

No longer attached to or under the direction of Hendon Police College, John Baldwin organized for escorts to be rehearsed on vacant airfields in the London area. 'Since we didn't have many vehicles directly posted to the SEG, cars and motorcycles were borrowed from traffic departments across London,' he explained. Having access to a runway allowed the group to perform formations at speed, and experiment with new techniques and routines in privacy. 'We used the opportunity to come up with new ideas for escorts,' added John. 'First, we'd walk through a manoeuvre on foot, carefully talking each action out loud for all team members to hear. Once we were happy, we'd then run the manoeuvre again, but this time on the bikes.' A large number of the group's formations were carefully developed and refined through this simple yet effective method.

One afternoon, while conducting routine practice, a light aircraft touched down on the runway. 'The pilot opened his side window and thrust out his arm holding up a set number of fingers. This was by no means a rude gesture!' laughed John, 'Rather it was a signal – an invitation. Each finger represented a spare seat.' He was offering the seats to any SEG officers who wanted to join him for a short flight. The number varied depending on how many of the seats were occupied, or had been removed and replaced with radio and navigational equipment, which the pilot was employed to test. These airborne jaunts were helpful tools for assessing manoeuvres from above and the 'research' trips proved popular with all officers.

Eventually word spread of the SEG's ingenious training methods. 'One afternoon, as we were conducting routine training at the airfield, three very senior police officers from Scotland Yard appeared,' said John. 'They were totally unannounced and unexpected. Their arrival was timed "conveniently" and apparently "coincidentally" with the landing of the aircraft.' Not realizing he was now under inspection, the pilot went straight into his routine, this time thrusting three fingers in their direction. 'One of the senior officers asked me what the hand gesture indicated,' explained John. 'Realizing that we'd be nobbled, I went about explaining how the "research" trips worked. The most senior of the three officers asked where the pilot was flying today and when I responded "the Isle of Wight", all three walked over to the plane and climbed aboard.'

When the airfield was in use, or sometimes just for a change of scenery, the group would occasionally relocate to Biggin Hill Raceway. Weeks would go by uneventfully as practice sessions both wet and dry were followed by rehearsals for future escorts and there were no pilots in sight. It was business as usual until one summer's afternoon, a couple of hours into practice, when someone rather exciting arrived.

Graham Hill OBE, the racing driver and Formula One World Champion, had been spotted by one of the group arriving at the racetrack. Shouldering up to Graham, who was admiring the police motorcycles at work, John asked cheekily: 'Would you fancy doing a lap with us?' To everyone's delight, Graham accepted enthusiastically. 'There was one problem though,' explained John. 'Graham's Formula One racing car had to drive at a minimum of sixty miles per hour otherwise the engine would stall. Compared to my 1960 MK II Jaguar, his was rocket propelled.'

In a scene befitting an episode of Top Gear, Graham launched off from the start line in his racing car. John, who was in a cumbersome and excessively heavy Jaguar, together with three of his men on motorcycles, also leapt into action like coiled springs. The Jag was quickly pushed to its limits, shuddering and screeching, 'but I just about managed to keep up with Graham', proclaimed John proudly. 'Propelled out of balance around corners, the car was forced to lean over and was near to the point of flipping a couple of times.' With Graham Hill leading the way, closely followed by the strained but skilfully-driven Jag, and surrounded by an escort and arrowhead of SEG motorcycles, the racing convoy must have been an incredible sight. Together, in formation, somehow, they survived several laps.

## The Space Race

The first escort of 1961 would launch the group to great heights and result in international publicity. John Baldwin and his well-trained team were to escort Yuri Gagarin – the first man in space and the biggest global celebrity of his time.

Gagarin, a Soviet military pilot and cosmonaut, had successfully reached beyond Earth's atmosphere. His bug-shaped capsule, the *Vostok* spacecraft, completed a single orbit of Earth on 12 April 1961. Victorious in the first leg of the space race – the competition between the United States and the Soviet Union to gain supremacy in spaceflights – Gagarin fast became an international celebrity and his country's hero.

Arriving in Britain in July, just three months after returning to Earth, he was met with huge public excitement, which was an absolute contrast to the reception the Soviet leaders received during their visit just a few years before. From the media perspective, Gagarin was one of the most interesting people in the world at the time. Paradoxically, success in space was also an indication that the Russians were one step closer to launching a nuclear weapon into the outer atmosphere, which, by all accounts, was not something to celebrate in the Western world.

Touching down at London City Airport, and after descending the air stair and walking on to the tarmac, Yuri Gagarin was greeted by government officials, together with an applauding crowd of fans and eager members of the press. An ostentatious white convertible Rolls Royce was parked just a few yards away, brandishing the number plate 'YG 1', which had been customized for his visit. After taking a seat in the rear of the car, the gleaming vehicle pulled away from the apron and out of the airport.

Six officers from the SEG, lined up neatly clear of the aircraft, sat on their newly-appointed Triumph Thunderbird motorcycles. The new bikes were to replace the older Triumphs, which had been purchased to escort Marshal Tito. Nicknamed 'Bath Tubs' due to the shape of the rear fairing, the gearing on them had been engineered specially for the group and offered better handling, particularly at low speeds, than their less-powerful predecessors.

As the Rolls Royce moved on to the public road, the motorcycles surrounded the vehicle with the box formation. They were bound for the Russian Embassy. Thousands of people had lined the pavements along the route and the mood of the crowd was electric. Men and women jumped to catch a glimpse of our out-of-this-world VIP and children cheered and waved. Yuri Gagarin was welcomed with open arms by an excited and entranced British public.

John Baldwin was also a fan. 'My two favourite escorts were Yuri Gagarin and Valentina Tereshkova, who was the first woman in space,' he said. 'Both were good fun, very friendly and the public reaction to them was incredible.'

Two short years after Gagarin's space-breaking mission, Lieutenant Valentina Tereshkova became the first woman in space and scored another big win for the Soviets. She'd carried out a solo flight spanning a period shy of three days, beginning on 16 June 1963. Just like Yuri, a few short months after returning from space, she had arrived in the UK for a celebratory tour and John Baldwin and his team had the honour of escorting her.

'One afternoon we took her to visit the birthplace of William Shakespeare in Stratford,' explained John. 'En route, one of the outriders slipped on roadside debris and lost control of his bike. He landed with his head on the pavement and his legs in the road.' When accidents like this happen, the convoy continues for security reasons and the fallen waits for a back up to help them. But Valentina had different ideas. 'Against my advice, Valentina insisted that the escort stop,' he said. 'To our surprise, she then got out of the car and sat holding his hand for a few minutes, until she was convinced he was OK.'

This was a landmark moment for the group. Not only was it the first accident during a run but it was also the first time they'd come face to face with their VIP in such an intimate way. 'Later that day Valentina invited us to the private gardens of the Russian Embassy,' added John. 'We joined her for tea and cake, spending time speaking with her privately.' Due to the ongoing Cold War, the embassy was entirely out of bounds to the British police and security agencies. The SEG's invitation to attend lunch in the grounds was therefore a milestone in diplomacy. The young astronaut had proved a big hit with the SEG. 'By the end of the day a couple of my blokes really fancied her,' said John with a glint in his eye.

## Escorting the Monarch, Her Majesty Queen Elizabeth II

By the middle of 1963, the SEG was being called upon on a regular basis and the group had taken on the additional low-key role of escorting important foreign government officials while in the UK on diplomatic business. In both 1961 and 1963, John had formed an escort for President Kennedy on two informal but high-profile visits, placing the group firmly in the spotlight.

The SEG's excellence was heralded in the national press, making the group evermore popular with the public. The SEG's reliability had been celebrated across government and its ability to enhance an event's levels of pomp and ceremony was being noted in British society, especially by the Household Cavalry who were the masters of pomp and ceremony.

With barely enough time to top up their fuel tanks following the visits of Tereshkova and President Kennedy, an unexpected but very welcome request for a prestigious escort was received. The group was to come together immediately at the behest of the royal household on behalf of Her Majesty. Aside from the coronation, this was the first time SEG had been charged with the great honour and responsibility of escorting the Monarch.

The purpose of the household's request was to seek additional police security during the state visit of the King and Queen of Greece. On 9 July 1963, King Paul of Greece, together with his wife Queen Frederica, arrived in the UK for what is often remembered as a controversial and turbulent stay. Despite the normal social protocols of a state visit, which is a moment of public celebration, the royal couple were received by angry crowds. Their protests pointed at the political situation in Greece – in particular, the detention of political prisoners, which had, for several months, been a matter of debate in the House of Commons.

The royal couple took residence, and to some extent sanctuary, at Claridge's Hotel in central London. The hotel was more than familiar to them as during the Second World War, the King of Greece, together with the King of Norway, and the King of Yugoslavia, had taken refuge there. On arrival at the hotel, under the close control of an SEG escort, the royal couple was to come face to face with the first of what would become a consistent crowd of protestors, many of whom were intent on ensuring the visit was a public calamity.

---

'Lesson for dealing with a crowd ahead: The leader observes unruly crowd ahead. At once he sends forward the leading six bikes who ride forward, dismount and make a passage for convoy. Immediately after the convoy has passed, the men then mount and re-join the escort falling in at the rear, the remaining bikes move forward.' – diary note from a retired SEG officer.

---

Despite the provision of a full SEG escort, it was, with the benefit of hindsight, clear that inadequate plans had been made to secure the various locations the couple were to visit during their stay in London. Consequently the angry mobs were able to get closer to the couple than was comfortable for those charged with their protection. A newspaper reported one sorry moment, when 'during their visit Queen Frederica was reported to have been forced to take refuge from the crowds in a residential house to avoid the angry crowds.'

On the second evening of their visit, HMQ and Queen Frederica, together with their husbands, attended a performance of *A Midsummer Night's Dream* at the Aldwych Theatre. A large number of protestors had gathered outside. In an attempt to calm and control them, foot duty police officers lined the pavements near to the entrance of the theatre. The royal car, which contained both Queens, received a single motorcycle escort provided by our very own John Baldwin. It was the first if its kind. As John explained: 'The royal household had refused any form of police escort for the Queen, preferring a plain-clothed police officer as a discreet bodyguard. On this occasion, I was accepted as a necessity due to the turmoil that had been predicted outside the theatre.'

The subject of inadequate security dominated discussion and debate in the Houses of Parliament for the prevailing weeks. Although a sad indictment of our government's inability to predict and plan for the unrest, the Metropolitan Police, especially the SEG, had once again come out as champions of the moment. The prestige of having escorted HMQ alone no doubt served John Baldwin well and helped him further develop and teach his team about the way of things to come. It was another proud day for those wearing the Metropolitan Police uniform.

## Operation Hope Not: The Funeral of Sir Winston Churchill

The morning of 30 January 1965 was rather typical for London during this time of year – cold, grey and crisp. For the SEG, routines remained the same as any other day; polish boots for a glass-like shine and check uniform is presentable. Read over escort route plan and remind oneself of key timings as noted in personal pocket book. Look over motorcycle for both presentational and mechanical reliability. Only this day wasn't going to be typical: rather it would signify the end of an incredible era.

Six days earlier, on Sunday, 24 January, Sir Winston Churchill died at his London home, 28 Hyde Park Gate in Kensington. With his wife, Lady Clementine Churchill, and immediate family by his side, the former prime

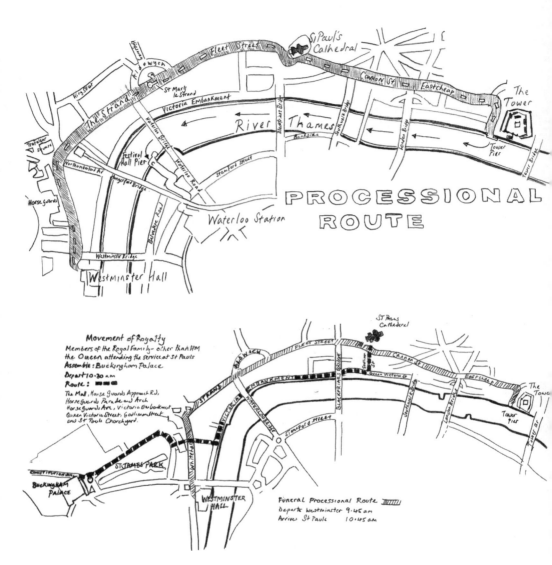

minister and war time leader passed away peacefully in his sleep. When news of his death reached the public, crowds gathered near his home to pay homage to Britain's greatest wartime leader. 'Tonight, our nation mourns the loss of the greatest man any of us have ever known,' declared Prime Minister Harold Wilson.

In 1958, HMQ instructed the Duke of Norfolk, in his capacity as Earl Marshal, to draw up a plan for a state funeral for Churchill. HMQ had made it known that he should be commemorated on a scale befitting his position in history. Following years of planning, Churchill's funeral had been meticulously organized, but preparation intensified in the weeks leading to his death. It had become clear that he was gravely ill. More than 1,000 officials were directly involved in delivering the funeral. Elements of the ceremony were incredibly complicated, requiring perfect timing and faultless coordination. For example, a Royal Airforce flyby, a 35-gun salute and the arrival of scores of heads of state at St Paul's Cathedral, including our own Queen, needed to be delivered flawlessly within a timeframe of just a handful of minutes.

None of this fazed John Baldwin. 'One afternoon I was summoned to the office of Commander Harry Crowdon at Bow Police Station,' said John. 'He showed me a list of about sixty kings, queens visiting heads of state and other high officials who were to attend the funeral. Harry asked me whether the SEG would be capable of escorting them all to St Paul's Cathedral. I said, "Yes Sir, it would be an honour."' John soon found himself sat at a desk next to Commander Crowdon. Drawn closely into the centre of the planning, this was to become a defining moment in John's career. 'The opportunity to work closely with Harry meant I got to see how much went into planning and then conducting an escort,' said John.

With only twenty-four officers experienced in working together as the SEG, John had to draw on his trusted and trained reserve list of men, known as the 'strappers'. The most complicated escort that day would be accompanying the foreign heads of state. Each of the fifteen VIPs were to gather in their individual limousines at the quadrangle in the grounds of Buckingham Palace at exactly 9.55 am. 'Every vehicle had its own motorcycle escort,' explained John. 'Our challenge was to escort the long convoy of limousines and have them arrive at St Paul's Cathedral at exactly the right time – not a minute early or a minute late.'

John and his team had to ensure that each head of state arrived no later than 10.22 am. This meant a 10.13 am departure from Buckingham Palace with 'absolutely no margin for error'. Without a single moment of delay, the SEG escort was required to dovetail smoothly into the rest of the funeral procession. Just a few short seconds after the final limousine, Queen Elizabeth The Queen Mother and members of the royal family were to arrive at the steps of St Paul's.

One of the heads of states attending the funeral was the President of Iceland Ásgeir Ásgeirsson. Well liked by his people, the president was known to be a calm and modest man; a well-read visionary and a diplomat by nature. During his tenure as president, he'd also become popular with British politicians. As a founding member of NATO (although Iceland did not declare war against Germany), and an important strategic ally during the Cold War, diplomatic channels between the UK and Iceland were vital. Churchill himself had visited Iceland during the war to meet with local officials, and the British troops who'd secured the island as a strategic North Atlantic base. Recognizing the long-term value of Iceland as an ally, Churchill had encouraged close relations with the North Atlantic nation. Iceland's role in Cold War diplomacy culminated in 1986, when they hosted a nuclear disarmament summit between President Ronald Reagan and Soviet Premier Mikhail Gorbachev.

The day after Churchill's death, Ásgeirsson made a statement to the people of Iceland:

> 'I will always remember the time when the British stood alone. All hope seemed small. But the British lion stood there focused and unmoving in the image of Sir Winston. I have often feared that we Icelanders did not fully realize how great the danger was for our western culture, the freedom of the individual, and the independence of the nation. As many other nations do, we owe Sir Winston a great debt of gratitude.'

On the morning of the funeral, the first leg of Ásgeirsson's journey was unescorted. Seated in a gleaming limousine, he was driven by his embassy chauffeur from his place of residence at the Westbury Hotel Mayfair to the busy quadrangle in the grounds of Buckingham Palace. On arrival, the normal routine of official greetings by the royal household staff was omitted. Instead, his vehicle was met by John Baldwin, together with his team of motorcycle escorts.

To save any potential confusion, at the request of the Lord Chamberlain's office, each of the VIP vehicles displayed a Green Crown windscreen sticker. The sticker, which also had a number, assisted the SEG officers in identifying each of the vehicles and placing them into the appropriate sequence in the convoy. With all vehicles in their place, and linked up with their respective motorcycle escort, the convoy moved off. In the few minutes of waiting between escorts, some of the SEG officers had spoken with the visiting dignitaries, many of whom were interested in the SEG. One officer recalled: 'At Churchill's funeral I met General Eisenhower. We passed the time of day together, whilst he was waiting for his car.'

Adding to the complexity of an already momentous challenge, over a million people turned out to line the pavements of the funeral route. There was a serious risk of onlookers spilling out from the pavement and creating obstacles for the escorted convoy. To add more pressure to the individual officers, any mishap whatsoever, whether that be a missing tunic button, dirty tyre or slip, slide or fall, would be seen by over 350 million people watching at home on their televisions from all corners of the world.

Despite being denied the opportunity to have a live dress rehearsal, John Baldwin and his team ensured that each of their vehicles arrived at St Paul's in a style befitting the event, and in clockwork precision time. The SEG's ability to deliver complex escorts such as this was well honed: perfected through meticulous practice and mindful self-reflection. The only way in which officers could communicate with each other was through hand signals and by reading the movement of each other's motorcycle; a method they'd perfected through multiple painstaking training days.

The following day, the *Daily Telegraph* wrote: 'Really, we do these things well in Britain. When we decide to honour one of our mighty dead, we honour him with fine dignity, with absolute simplicity and with astonishing precision.' That 'astonishing precision' was largely due to a handful of individuals of which John was key. 'That day really helped launch my own career,' he said. 'It was not only a great honour for me and the rest of the team, but it also gave the grounding the SEG needed to become a permanent fixture and take on a wider range of escorts.' Commander Harry Crowdon had witnessed first hand what the SEG was capable of doing, and from that moment on became its biggest champion, pushing the group forward, advertising its capability, and elevating its status within the senior ranks of the Metropolitan Police.

'Operation Hope Not', which was the codename for Churchill's funeral, had happened and it had, unquestionably, secured the future of the SEG. It is no coincidence that as high-profile events such as this one took place in London, police motorcycle escort teams began to emerge around the world, often modelled on the methods of the SEG. John Baldwin and his team understood that they weren't just setting the standard for their peers in other countries, they were leading it, as they continue to do to this day.

## The State Visit of King Faisal of Saudi Arabia

The assassination of President John F. Kennedy in November 1963 resulted in protective escorts all over the world increasing their security measures and being on even higher alert than before. In what has become the most famous assassination of all time, Kennedy was shot fatally inside his presidential motorcade, while in the care and protection of his security team. In the UK, the SEG and colleagues across the security community, began a process of thinking through additional countermeasures in the event of an attack. The JFK shooting was used by security teams as a case study globally, and helped form counter-attack training exercises and procedures.

By the late 1960s, the world was beginning to feel a little less safe. Inspired by the civil rights marches in the US – championed by Martin Luther King Jr (who himself would be assassinated in public in 1968) – protests were becoming more frequent in the UK, especially in Northern Ireland. Violent clashes between the security forces and Northern Irish activists were increasingly common. By the middle of 1968, these conflicts led to serious injuries and triggered the start of a period that is commonly referred to as 'the Troubles'. Peace was fragile and fast fading.

The SEG continued to work with royal families from around the globe, and in 1967 it was called upon to escort King Faisal of Saudi Arabia, who, according to popular myth, had brought with him to the UK his personal foot warmer, a young boy whose primary purpose was to rub the king's feet when required. Anti-communist and a close ally of the US, King Faisal was said to have worked hard to maintain close relationships with all western nations. His influence in the Middle East as a pro-western leader, a modernizer, and someone who refused political ties with the Soviet Union had made him an important ally to the UK.

During an official visit to Buckingham Palace for an audience with HMQ, King Faisal was reported to have given Her Majesty an extremely valuable diamond necklace, which was an unorthodox but no doubt very welcome gesture. The SEG was on full security alert during his stay. Although popular with many belonging to the political class in the West, the king ruled in a region experiencing human turmoil, violence and political unrest. Consequently, his own life was always at significant risk. Thankfully, from a security perspective, his visit to Britain was uneventful. Sadly, however, some years later in 1975, having recently returned to his own country from a visit to the US, he was murdered by gunshot, by a member of his own family.

**President Richard Nixon**

Richard Nixon, 37th President of the United States, arrived in the UK in February 1969. 'The entire world was watching', said John Baldwin. 'Perhaps the finest hour during my time with the SEG was the visit of President Nixon.' Although he is renowned for the Watergate scandal and being the only president to resign from office, at the time of his visit he was heralded as a world statesman who was championing the West's fight during the Cold War. It would be the first of several visits to Britain in his capacity of president. News coverage of his trip reached all corners of the world.

Nixon was determined to end the Vietnam War during his presidency. However, after instructing a rapid withdrawal of US troops from the country, an outbreak of violence erupted on the southern border with Cambodia, threatening the chances of peace. With the enemy losing ground and control in Vietnam, communist Vietnamese troops had developed strongholds inside Cambodia. The sanctuaries were used to regain strength, launch attacks, and build a springboard from which to seize control of Cambodia's capital, Phnom Penh.

In response to the enemy Vietnamese tactics, and despite attempts at a peaceful conclusion, Nixon increased military campaigns in Cambodia, along the southern Vietnam border. Although the decision was seen by many as controversial, by the time of his next visit to the UK in October 1970, Nixon was able to herald the operation as a success.

Furthermore, during the first few years of his presidential term, he'd come face-to-face with Cold War turmoil, eventually culminating in border clashes between China and the Soviet Union, Gaddafi overthrowing the Libyan Monarchy, expelling British and American embassy personnel, and aligning himself with Russia. Although seven years had passed since the Cuban Missile Crisis, the fear of nuclear war hadn't waned in the public consciousness. The US influence on restoring peace and security was seen as essential by most western countries. Many thought Nixon was exactly the sort of leader the international stage needed for these troubled times.

Nixon's public address to the UK focused on the urgent need for world peace. A desire for total alignment between the UK and US was at an all-time high, so the president's visit was essential in the development of policy between the two countries and for helping to cement Anglo-American public opinion.

Once again, John Baldwin and his group were in the spotlight. John had been given the job of forming the team, planning the routes, and riding the lead bike in the Nixon escort. One of the president's appointments saw the SEG escort him to Chequers,, the country retreat of Prime Minister Harold Wilson. Chequers Court, as it is officially known, is located at the foot of the Chiltern Hills in Buckinghamshire. The roads leading to the great house are ancient, winding and barricaded by thick hedges. The president travelled in a newly-appointed black, armoured limousine. The vehicle, which had been built specially following lessons learnt from JFK's assassination, had been shipped in from the US. As he concluded his visit, Nixon asked to speak to John, who recalled that:

'We shook hands and had a short conversation on the airstrip, moments before he departed in his presidential plane. He explained how impressed he'd been with my team. He took great interest in our method of working, noting that it was very different from what he was used to in the US. After a couple of questions from him, followed by answers from me, he looked me straight in the eyes and said: "Those roads near Chequers were mighty windy and thin. How do you do it so quickly?"'

It was obvious to John that the president had found moments of the escort to be rather exciting. A photograph capturing the exchange of words between John and President Nixon made headline news. But it did more than make the papers; it triggered a tradition of the VIP shaking hands with the officer in charge, or lead motorcyclist, of SEG. It is a tradition unique to the SEG, and one that hundreds of visiting dignitaries have continued to this day.

Shortly after Nixon's departure, a reputable TV company approached the SEG asking if it could make a film about the escorts that had taken place during the visit. John was enthusiastic as he saw this as a good opportunity to reach out to the public and help them understand the group's work. Sadly for John and his team, a senior officer from New Scotland Yard refused the request with a written note that said: 'I am not supporting the creation of a personality cult.' The idea was buried.

## The Investiture of the Prince of Wales

The investiture of the Prince of Wales took place at Caernarfon Castle, in the north west of Wales, on 1 July 1969. The event, which signified the formal creation of the title 'Prince of Wales' for the Queen's eldest son Prince Charles, was attended by hundreds and observed by millions. Unsurprisingly, with so many royals in attendance, it commanded the highest levels of security. Threat assessments would have concluded that the event presented a series of unique vulnerabilities caused in part by the location. So far away from the well-established security architecture of London, precautions would need to be taken to ensure that Prince Charles and his guests wouldn't become an attractive target for terrorist groups.

This was the final SEG escort of the 1960s. 'It required a huge number of bikes and significant planning and coordination,' explained John. 'We employed a total of sixty officers on motorcycles to provide perimeter security, and a small number of escorts for the prince and other members of the royal family.' Twenty-two of the motorcyclists were members of the SEG, ten from the MPT, and the remainder were made up out of known and trusted officers from the traffic department.

Several teams were formed: some had responsibility patrolling the surrounding roads while others were convoy escorts. The entire operation was planned several months in advance with many SEG officers visiting the location and testing routes weeks prior to the actual event. Several days ahead of the investiture, the motorcycle contingent travelled to Wales to begin rehearsals and practise their routines for the big day. The sixty officers, who were reporting from various locations across London, had arranged to rendezvous at the Triumph motorcycle factory located in the village of Meriden between Coventry and Birmingham. PC Ray Young, who served with the MPT between 1965 and 1969, explained why: 'The factory was en route to Wales and the owners of Triumph were keen on having us all line up outside the factory for a marketing photo. It was great fun seeing all the bikes together at their birthplace.' The sixty motorcycles then remained together for the rest of the journey to Caernarfon, with 'the MPT riding at the helm in arrow formation for much of the route,' explained Ray.

Back in London, Prime Minister Wilson expressed concerns about the security threat to Charles, and had considered requesting that the 20-year-old prince cancel plans to spend time at Aberystwyth University prior to the ceremony. Directing the Metropolitan Police to take additional caution, officers from Special Branch were sent to work closely with the Welsh police ahead of the ceremony. A special intelligence unit was set up specifically for the event. Despite these extra measures, on 4 February 1969 Wilson wrote to the Home Secretary to say: 'The security position, as I understand it, still gives cause for concern; and we must be as sure as we can that all possible precautions are taken.' The letter continued: 'I want to feel confident that, if necessary, I can advise the Queen that in the Government's opinion the whole programme between now and July can go forward without significant risk of any untoward interruption.' At one point, the prime minister even went so far as to suggest that the investiture be cancelled. However, it went ahead as scheduled.

On the eve of the ceremony, two men from a Welsh extremist group accidently blew themselves up while carrying bombs intended to disrupt the investiture. Furthermore, classified files released in the early 1990s suggest that the Russian KGB had planned to blow up a bridge close to Caernarfon Castle weeks before the event in the hope of embarrassing and damaging the reputation of the security services. The reason for their change of heart is unknown but may have been due to a lack of opportunity thanks to security at the castle.

Despite the efforts of would-be disrupters, and thanks to the good work of the police, especially the SEG, the military and security services, the investiture followed through entirely as planned.

**Triumph Thunderbird (1959-1967 approx).** The bike displayed below is a conventional traffic duty motorcycle. Produced in many variations, the SEG employed the 650cc motorcycle with great success. The group bike had the panniers, unsightly radio and double headlight fairing removed to improve its overall elegance and agility. The later addition of a bathtub-like rear fairing provided extra splash protection on rainy days. Extremely easy to ride at low speeds and with lively acceleration, the bike handled well for both ceremonial and conventional policing purposes.

# The 1970s

## Preparing For a New Range of Threats

Flower power walked a stairway to heaven and the Beatles buzzed off. Disco dominated the dance floors and men and women strutted their stuff in floor-skimming flares and pounded the pavements of London's increasingly multicultural streets in platform shoes. When we look back at this decade, it's easy to forget how hostile times were. The SEG was all too aware.

The decade was to present the group with the greatest period of change in its history so far. It was the start of an era dominated by high security caused by clear and direct threats, and with this came new leadership, new mandates, new staff, new bikes, new everything!

Post-war optimism about the UK's strength as a global power was waning, and national security was beginning to dominate public consciousness. Equally, conversations about security in the closed meeting rooms of Whitehall commanded a new sense of urgency. The question was what to do about it. The decade ahead was to witness unprecedented levels of domestic terrorism and extremism.

'Operation Foot' was the codename given to the mass expulsion of 105 Russian spies from UK soil in 1971. During the late 1960s, espionage against the UK's interests had risen to an all-time high. A number of Russian 'intelligence successes', including the recruitment of well-placed British citizens, had put the British security service, MI5, and the Metropolitan Police Special Branch, on full alert. The government assessed that the increased levels of espionage had caused significant damage to British interests. Although much of the 'spying' wasn't public knowledge, awareness of the nuclear threat had been popularized through various documentaries and films about the Cold War, and, in particular, the Cuban Missile Crisis of 1962. Some of the key events are as follows:

Despite the encouraging advice of Led Zeppelin in *Stairway To Heaven* – 'There are two paths you can go by, but in the long run, there's still time to change the road you're on' – by the middle of 1970, the Irish Republican Army (IRA) had selected a path of violence. Between 1970 and 1972, more than 500 people lost their lives due to The Troubles in Northern Ireland. By the time IRA terrorism tactics ended in 1998 with the signing of the Good Friday Agreement, more than 3,600 people had been killed with as many as 50,000 seriously injured. Numbers vary, but in the region of 10,000 bombs were detonated, hundreds in the UK mainland, with scores upon scores in London.

In September 1971, Employment Secretary Robert Carr escaped injury after being the target of a twin bomb attack at his home in Barnet, Hertfordshire. The bombs had been planted by the Angry Brigade, a recently-formed left-wing revolutionary group. These anarchists were thought to have planted twenty-five bombs between 1970 and 1972, when they were successfully disbanded with key individuals arrested.

A year later in Munich, eleven members of the Israeli Olympic team were taken hostage, and eventually killed, by the Palestinian terrorist group Black September. Throughout the 1970s, Palestinian terrorist groups would continue to increase the volume of hostage taking (which included hijacking passenger aeroplanes) and initiate terrorist attacks in Europe and beyond.

Violent, organized crimes were also prevalent in London and were quickly capturing the attention of the government. Competition between criminal groups led to power battles, with some arming themselves in an attempt at gaining a lead. Unfortunately, the early 1970s also saw a degree of police corruption, especially within departments such as the Flying Squad, which were responsible for investigating serious, violent crimes. Many commentators argue that although the corruption was isolated to a tiny number of officers, it helped energize a growth in organized crimes, particularly armed robbery. By 1973, newly-appointed Commissioner of the Metropolitan Police, Robert Mark, was charged to take action and told his subordinates 'the basic test of a decent police force is that it catches more criminals than it employs.' Mark quickly launched an aggressive anti-corruption drive, which eventually led to the early retirement or resignation of ninety officers in 1973 alone. Internal investigations continued throughout the decade leading to scores of high-profile prosecutions of police officers.

The SEG was increasingly mindful of an organized crime group kidnapping an escort for ransom. Although it was unlikely, there was also the possibility of an 'insider' tipping off a criminal gang and passing on names, routes and timings of a run. This meant that a heightened culture of secrecy, and a need-to-know basis, was becoming the norm within the group. Furthermore, with an increased threat to dignitaries from foreign terrorist groups, increased espionage, a clear threat from the IRA and a heightened understanding of terrorist tactics overseas, SEG operational tradecraft needed to change and modernize. The challenge for the Metropolitan Police security teams, and particularly SEG, was to increase security whilst maintaining the exquisitely-high level of ceremonial presentation that had become expected of them.

The security community is very much like any other organization or team – it is a product of its past experience. It is almost entirely shaped by lessons learnt from former challenges, and while aware of the need to evolve, it is institutionally reluctant to do so. Despite the very best intentions to think, plan and prepare for what's next, it is occasionally caught out by surprise. However, unlike many organizations which operate in predictable climates, regulated and governed by international laws and codes of practice, the security community is confronted with adversaries who are entirely unpredictable. They write their own rules and operate well outside of the constraints of law.

MI5, Special Branch as well as several other contributing government agencies, worked hard to conduct threat assessments, which in turn would inform those charged with protecting dignitaries. Such assessments can be difficult to build, and from an intelligence perspective, the challenge to gather crucially-important insights was substantial. The Provisional Irish Republican Army (PIRA), which saw themselves as the successor to the IRA following a split in the movement, was fast becoming considered the main threat, but their secretive and well-organized methods made them hard to second guess.

Faced with these circumstances, there were a number of ways the SEG could prepare for the turbulent and uncertain future ahead. The first option was to do nothing, and rely on experience and existing procedures. This might be an option for some perhaps, but not for such a conscientious and professional outfit.

The second would be to study the enemy and ask questions such as: what is their motivation, capability and final goal? How do they intend on achieving those goals? And do they have the capacity to achieve them? The answers to such questions allow the security community to build plans, and rehearse specific scenarios, which are adjusted depending on how intelligence agencies and specialist police units, such as Special Branch, determine how an attack might take place. The British security community has always been very good at expecting the unexpected and for this we owe them much credit.

The third is to mirror yourself, which is a technique often favoured by the military whilst at war. Essentially they ask, how would we attack us? This is used when there is a lack of specific knowledge about the adversary, but a threat is known to exist. The downside of this approach is the risk of continuous escalation and doubling up of one's own security posture – think of a US presidential motorcade. As the SEG knows instinctively, too many layers of physical security can create insecurity.

The fourth way is perhaps the most challenging, but also the most effective. It demands a willingness to embrace uncertainty. To do so requires honing the intellectual skill of hypothesis building; in this case to imagine a wide range of possible attack scenarios, and plan for them accordingly. However, no matter how good the SEG might become at hypothesizing and developing responses, the hard truth is that many of its adversaries were capable of employing surprising, sophisticated and sometimes ingenious methods. This meant that if an attack were to take place, there would almost certainly be an element of unpredictability to it. Officers needed to develop high levels of vigilance and be capable of scanning their surroundings at speed, analyzing suspicious activity on the spot, and making instant, and potentially critical decisions, all while safely operating their vehicles through London's demanding traffic.

When the security community prepares for uncertainty, teams are 'exercised' through a wide range of complex, challenging and unpredictable scenarios. One of the aims is to help individuals form habits of mind that allow them to balance 'procedures', which have been developed through years of experience, against a necessity to think on their feet. Often individuals and teams in this community will make decisions independently of the prevailing norms, so they must be willing, able and decisive in thinking outside the box. It is, of course, all summed up in the telling motto of the Special Air Service (SAS) – 'Who dares wins.'

## Things were slow to change

'It really wasn't until the attempted kidnapping of Princess Anne in 1974, followed by the attack on the EL AL aircrew in 1978, that we started to move away from straightforward ceremonial duties, and towards becoming a high-security escort group,' explained one SEG officer who had served during this period.

One might ask why change in the methodology for protecting dignitaries wasn't initiated immediately. The security landscape had certainly changed and was in full view of its observers. But as with many great challenges, you can only guess how to take it on when you're in the midst of it and then it's too late to ponder so you can only react. At that point, it's all down to fight or flight and there's rarely time to think. The very best we can hope for is to learn lessons from those instances. However the SEG also faced resistance to change from those who felt it would move the group away from its original purpose. The group had been set up with the primary function of supporting high-profile ceremonial events. Although security was a feature, protocol had been firmly established to allow the public as much access to the VIP as possible.

In the absence of high-security escort procedures, specialist training, appropriate equipment, armoured vehicles, new directives from the good and the great, and so on, the SEG developed its own methods to remain sharp and keep the dignitaries safe. Never underestimate the ingenuity and resourcefulness of a police officer when placed in a corner. Hidden out of sight, but working feverously behind the scenes, specialist police units supported SEG escorts to ensure that attacks were prevented, and, in the unfortunate event of an attack, that the good guys would be as prepared as possible.

## Emperor Hirohito of Japan

On the final day of his visit, moments before departing UK soil, Emperor Hirohito of Japan, short and somewhat plainly dressed, with hat absentmindedly in hand, inspected the SEG officers on the airstrip at Heathrow. It's difficult to imagine what was going through the minds of the team. The man, who walked by looking them up and down, was the emperor in power during the Japanese air attack on Pearl Harbor some thirty years before.

More than 2,400 Americans died during the attacks, with another 1,178 wounded, many with life-changing injuries. Approximately 13,000 British soldiers, and over 2000 civilians also died in Japanese wartime camps. Thousands were tortured and suffered humiliation, and many died from disease or starvation. Following Japan's defeat in the Second World War, the question of who was responsible for the atrocities was much disputed. Many commentators suggested that all key warfare decisions were made by military leaders without the emperor's knowledge or approval. Others disagreed. This visit, some three decades later, was important. Japan was a powerful democratic country and our closest ally geographically to communist China. Whatever the politics of the past, it was now an important ally to the West. The emperor's visit demonstrated a huge leap in commitment and trust in that relationship.

Emperor Hirohito, 69, and his 68-year-old wife, Empress Kōjun, started their four-day state visit at Gatwick Airport on 5 October 1971. A landmark in history, this was the first time a Japanese emperor had visited the UK, or indeed ever entered Europe. The visit had been initiated by an invitation from HMQ. A private train was provided to bring him from the airport to London Victoria, where he was met at the platform's edge by the Queen, members of the royal family, and an entourage of government officials. Travelling from the station to Buckingham Palace in a royal horse-drawn carriage, he was also seen by the public. Few waved but many others stood silent. Some turned their back as he passed. In amongst those crowds were a number of survivors and former prisoners of war.

Despite the unwelcoming public the emperor's visit took place peacefully, thanks in part to the security surrounding him. On returning him to the airport, John Baldwin recalled Hirohito's final moments before leaving British soil. 'We had been asked to stand lined up so the emperor could meet us. We'd been told that he was extremely impressed with us all.' John and his men lined up just a few metres away from the aeroplane. 'The emperor quickly walked up to us, halting just before me. He looked up at me, and in a serious voice started to compliment the work of my team.' Moments before this, the emperor had requested that a photo be taken with him standing with the SEG officers and their bikes. 'We were all most surprised,' explained John. 'Before climbing the steps to his aircraft, he thanked us once more and requested that the photos be sent to his private office in Japan. We later heard news, through diplomatic channels, that the photo had gained a home on the emperor's desk.'

The emperor had been so impressed with SEG, that on returning to Tokyo he ordered the chief of the Japanese police to train his own motorcycle protection team using SEG methods. The emperor's request culminated in a team of Japanese motorcycle officers being sent to the UK to undergo SEG training. And the tradition continues to this day. John remembered the first group of Japanese arriving at Hendon Police College: 'We arrived at the college to meet with the Japanese officers and show them a few tricks of the trade. They were all stood neatly in line waiting eagerly for us. It was a lovely experience, but we spent about ten minutes bowing to each other before we could get going.'

## A Royal Honeymoon

In 1973, when Anne, the Princess Royal, married Captain Mark Phillips, the press were eager to find out where they were going to spend the first night of their honeymoon. 'The palace were equally determined that they shouldn't find out,' explained one retired SEG officer. The group was enlisted in the hope it could help the newlyweds retain their privacy.

'We rode to one of the lesser-known gates at Buckingham Palace, where we met with the royal couple's chauffeur-driven car,' recalled the officer. However after leaving the palace, a couple of journalists picked up their tail in their own cars. 'We proceeded to escort the couple to their final destination, The White Lodge, Richmond Park, once home of Queen Mary. After the first set of traffic lights we lost the pursuing vehicles. As far as I know, it was only afterwards that the press reported where they had stayed.'

Although this wasn't the first of the royal runs, it was a sign of things to come. The royal household had come to trust the SEG, and the benefits of the smooth and time-efficient escorts were well known and appreciated by an increasing number of the royal family.

## The retirement of Chief Superintendent John Baldwin

John retired from the police in 1973. Despite rocketing from constable to chief superintendent in record time, he had always kept his boots firmly on the ground. His foremost concern was always for the welfare of his officers. He understood that if the *esprit de corps* was strong, his team would deliver excellence, and he was right. During John's tenure, he instilled values into the group's DNA which helped form its enviable, and rather unique culture and style; this included humour and playfulness, personal and professional discipline, a passion for precision, total trust in the team, openness, inclusiveness, and respect for those it charged to protect.

The SEG had experienced incredible levels of popularity, and indeed public fame, under John's leadership. There were times when officers more senior to John had gently, or sometimes aggressively, edged their way into the group to benefit from its success. John diplomatically managed them all, creating powerful champions for the group, rather than enemies. In return, he was given the respect, trust and independence he needed to lead and develop the SEG through some tremendously challenging times. John Baldwin did so much more than simply lay the foundations of the world's finest escort group. He formed its personality and culture. The standards and style he instilled remain today. John was one of those exceptional people that you rarely have the privilege to meet, but when you do, you know you're in wise company and safe hands.

A man in search of a new adventure, on retirement John took up a position as the head of security at Guy's Hospital in London, where he spent the remainder of his working years.

The newly-appointed inspector in charge of SEG was Derek Gosse, who would oversee the beginning of what was to become an intense couple of years for the group. Between 1973 and 2000 there would be a further five inspectors directly in charge of the SEG. Each of their stewardships would steer the SEG through considerable change.

This included change to the security environment in which they worked, change to the breadth of their responsibilities and range of customers, change to the operational tradecraft, and change to whom they reported. A number of high-profile security incidents doubled the pace of the change, starting with the attempted kidnap of HRH Princess Anne.

## Attempted Kidnap of Princess Anne

'Public figures have always been in danger to some degree,' admitted Princess Anne in an interview with celebrated TV host, Michael Parkinson.

'Queen Victoria had five attempts during her reign. Most of them were solo attackers.' On 20 March 1974, Princess Anne and her husband, Captain Mark Phillips, were travelling along the Mall in the back of their chauffeur-driven car when it was forced to a sudden stop by a white Ford Escort driven by Ian Ball. The princess was without an escort. Indeed, the only protection she had was a lone police officer, Inspector James Deaton, who was sitting next to the chauffeur in the front passenger seat of the limousine.

The incident that followed was to make headline news around the world. Ian Ball exited his car and approached the royal vehicle. Inspector Deaton jumped out to speak with Ball, thinking he was an irate motorist. Ball immediately fired at Deaton, striking his chest and knocking him to the floor. Deaton managed to fire a single return shot but missed. His second attempt failed as his gun jammed. In a brave effort to distract Ball, the royal driver attempted to intervene but was also shot.

Ball's plan was to kidnap the princess and hold her to ransom. Now he focused his attention on trying to convince the 23-year-old, and the only daughter of the Queen, to exit her limousine. 'Having shot my police officer and chauffeur, we had a discussion about what we were or were not going to do,' explained Anne. 'He said I had to go with him. I said I didn't want to. I was scrupulously polite, 'cos I thought, silly to be too rude at this stage.' Another police officer arrived on the scene but didn't notice that Ball was armed or that two individuals had already been shot. He too was shot.

In the words of Princess Anne 'the tedious discussion continued for several minutes' until eventually Ball decided to try and pull her out of the vehicle. She chuckled how she recalled that a member of the public came over to have a look. 'He came all the way across the road, looked in through the window, and he went "Hmm, so it is", and turned and he walked all the back, wandering off down the Mall.'

Ball and the princess continued to tussle until she complained that 'the back of my dress split; the shoulders went out of it and that was his most dangerous moment. I lost my rag at that stage.' Eventually the struggle culminated with Captain Mark Phillips pulling one of her arms and Ball pulling the other. A few more minutes passed. By this time, the second police officer, who was lying on the ground injured, had managed to radio for urgent assistance.

Following a failed, but brave, intervention of passerby Ron 'the Geezer' Russell, a former heavyweight boxer who punched Ball in the back of the head, the police arrived on the scene. Seeing the officers, the princess shouted 'Come on, now's your chance!' At the sight of the police, Ball fled into St James's Park but was quickly apprehended and smothered by the police, or as the princess described them, 'the local rugby team'. By the end of the ordeal, Ball had fired off a total of six shots from his two pistols, leaving four people seriously injured. Fortunately, all survived and neither Princess Anne nor her husband were harmed.

Despite claiming to have lost her rag, the princess remained calm at all times. She had decided that her best course of action was to do everything she could to remain inside the vehicle. In hindsight, the decision was to prove very wise. At the conclusion of her interview with Parkinson, she said: 'Perhaps the greatest danger seems to be the lone nutter who has just enough to pull it together. That said, if anyone was seriously intent on wiping one out, it would be very easy to do.'

As Deaton, who later became chief superintendent in charge of royalty protection explained: 'This was the 1970s. There was very little training, a little bit on firearms, but that was about it. Nothing had ever happened. The furthest thing from my mind was somebody that was going to do us any harm.' At this time, the majority of royal movements in motorcars were undertaken in the presence of single police officers. 'The vehicles weren't even fitted with radios,' added Deaton. 'You were completely alone and without any mechanism to communicate. If you fitted a radio to a car it came with long aerials – it was deemed on a royal car that it would spoil the look of it.'

Later, Ball claimed his ultimate aim was to raise awareness to the lack of funding and support for those with mental health issues. He said: 'I am only sorry that I frightened the princess. There is one good thing coming out of this: you will have to improve on her protection.' He subsequently pleaded guilty to charges of attempted murder and attempted kidnap. It is believed that he remains in prison under the Mental Health Act to this day.

Ball was right in needing to improve security and the event led to a much-needed overhaul of how the royal family, and visiting dignitaries, were protected. The SEG was to be found willingly at the forefront, leading the change.

Dress: to attain an even higher standard of smartness strict attention to detail is of paramount importance, viz:

1. Correct fitting of all clothing including protective head gear
2. Highly polished helmets
3. Highly polished boots
4. Boots laced in uniform manner throughout the group
5. Jackets buttoned up to the neck

Deportation: From the outset team spirit should be encouraged. A code of conduct:

1. Alert and upright in riding position
2. 100% concentration whilst riding or standing by machines
3. Talking to members of the public, press or to one another is strictly forbidden within public view
4. When dismounted, the group should stand to attention unless otherwise ordered by the officer in charge or leader – extract from the SEG handbook.

## Arming the Group

In January 1976, Sergeant Jock Shields stood down from his position at the SEG, following a term of exactly ten years. During that period, he'd contributed volumes to the group. With an eye for both precision and presentation, he had written the first SEG internal handbook, turning well-honed working practices into operational guidance. The handbook, which reached scores of pages, delivered well-thought out advice on escort formations, motorcycle inspection, dress and deportment, and a detailed explanation of each role and rank. The attention to detail helped protect, experience and inform the new generation of the standards achieved in the past. The continuity provided by the handbook proved invaluable in the period of change ahead of the SEG. For his achievements in the police, especially while serving with the SEG, Sergeant Shields was awarded the British Empire Medal.

By the start of 1976, the SEG had introduced both cars and firearms into many of its escorts. This was a major change for a previously-unarmed team, which had relied solely on the use of motorcycles for twenty-three years.

The news that concealed revolvers were to be carried on most runs was well received by the group. Many of the officers were already trained in guns and carried a valid firearms certificate. At the time, however, the subject of arming the Metropolitan Police was controversial and generally unwelcome in the eyes of the public. SEG was mindful and respectful of this. 'All weapons had to be worn inside our uniforms so as not to concern anyone,' explained a retired officer.

On the highest-risk escorts, motorcycles alone were considered too vulnerable as they were too exposed. Thus, police cars were added into the fold. The Rover 3.5 was the vehicle of choice and occasionally the Triumph 2000. Large, powerful and speedy saloon cars provided a better shield for officers in the event of an attack and they could also be used to ram would-be attackers. The introduction of cars meant they could carry more armed officers and this extra manpower could deliver additional firepower in the event of an attack.

Despite the new high-risk responsibility, SEG lacked a car fleet of its own. As one retired officer divulged, the group had to beg and borrow from traffic garages. 'This wasn't always easy, since the garages were reluctant to release their spare vehicles. At times, we were borrowing up to a dozen vehicles each day.' Between 1976 and the end of 1977, the lack of dedicated vehicles meant that some escorts, which would have normally had the SEG in a lead role, were handed over to Special Branch. The most notable of these was the state visit of President Jimmy Carter in May 1977. The visit, and the president's schedule, were kept as low key as possible.

By the late 1970s the SEG had taken over the role of escorting 'Category A' prisoners. These were individuals identified to be high risk, such as IRA terrorists and notorious violent criminals. The new responsibility meant the SEG escorted prison vans between the prison and court hearings across London and the south east of England. For a brief period of time the SEG was, at the request of the magistrates, also responsible for securing the actual court when prisoners were inside.

'Cat As had previously been escorted by the Special Patrol Group (SPG)[1] but their method was inefficient, using a very large number of officers,' explained Richard 'Rick' Johnson, a retired SEG chief who led the group between November 1976 and March 1981. Superintendent Johnson was a veteran of the prestigious Grenadier Guards and considered to be a trusted

---

1. The SPG was responsible for policing serious public disorder and crimes that could not be dealt with by local division. It was disbanded in 1987.

hand. Prior to joining the SEG he'd worked as a uniformed sergeant in Brixton, where'd he'd had responsibility for court security (and this is also where'd he'd developed his relationship with the SPG). He'd then transferred for a brief spell as a detective to Commissioner Robert Mark's internal corruption team.

'I was asked if we'd take over SPG duties with the assistance of the firearms unit. I gratefully accepted the work,' said Johnson. Extra responsibilities were welcomed as they helped the SEG justify becoming a permanent team, which was something that had been considered ever since the workload had started to increase in the late 1960s. Taking on the prisoner escorts also gave the SEG the opportunity to practise new methods, which combined cars with motorcycles. Apparently, the prisoners were also happy with the change. 'On one occasion the prisoners, I believe IRA, complained about the terrible driving of the SPG, saying that the driver had nearly turned over the van,' explained another retired officer.

Some years later the SEG would learn, in a public court hearing, that the IRA had planned a rescue attempt on a convoy using machine guns. It was unclear as to whether the rescue operation went ahead or not. Whatever the case the group had no knowledge of such an attempt. On another occasion, while handing over an IRA arrestee to the prison service, the prisoner is reported to have said to the officers handling him: 'I will do more harm inside this prison than outside. I'm an economic terrorist now.'

Another change in the SEG was the reliance on leapfrogging during escorts. Leapfrogging was an extremely effective system, which had been used regularly in conventional traffic duties while escorting heavy, unusually-long, wide and dangerous loads. The technique involved motorcycles leaping ahead of the convoy to stop and control traffic at busy or potential hazardous junctions. Timing was everything. 'One didn't want to hold back traffic for an unnecessarily long period of time, but you did need to allow enough time to ensure you could probably clear and control the junction prior to the arrival of the escort,' explained a retired SEG officer.

Although leapfrogging had been employed by the group on occasion in the 1960s, it wasn't required or suited to ceremonial escorts, since traffic junctions had typically been controlled by foot duty officers. However, as the group started to take on lower-key escorts, including an increasing number of escorts for members of the royal family (such as moving the Princess Royal to her honeymoon destination), the technique became more popular.

'Leapfrogging meant we didn't need to use the valuable time of foot duty, and nor did we need to inform the wider police network of our routes and timings,' said an SEG officer. 'This kept our escorts as private as possible, something that became increasingly important as the years went on.' Additionally, it allowed the group to change route while in escort (since they were no longer dependent on foot duty officers) and the overall speed of an escort could be increased or decreased, if needed.

## Royals Aboard!

By 1977, a number of royals were requesting, and casually using, the services of the SEG for low-key events and public duties. The majority of these escorts were done 'off the record' since the SEG hadn't yet received a mandate to do them. Furthermore, HMQ was, at the time, believed to be concerned about the use of police time. It was also thought that she was concerned at members of the royal family holding up public traffic any more than was absolutely necessary. The preferred method of moving a royal between regular duties had been to use a chauffeur-driven limousine, in the company of an officer from Royalty Protection.

The method of escort varied and adapted as the group gained feedback from their royal passengers, and discussed the pros and cons of their latest run with colleagues. The rulebook was, in effect, thrown out of the window for these jobs and new escorting techniques were tried, tested, reviewed and developed. There was however one rule that couldn't be broken and that was the cardinal sin of arriving early at the final destination. Early was much worse than late. Since the escorts now had to contend with junctions and traffic, predicting the timing of a route became much more challenging.

One senior SEG officer recalled that 'an inspector from Royalty Protection suggested we experiment using motorcycles to move Princess Alexandra. Gaining approval from my commander it was agreed.' This type of movement required the use of leapfrogging and, to maintain operational flexibility, the route was not set in advance, which meant that the convoy could change direction at any time (always having surveyed the route previously). The convoy would travel at a steady pace while the leapfrogging bikes would have to reach much higher speeds. The new technique commanded extremely high levels of concentration, an uncanny skill for reading traffic conditions, and the ability to think well ahead of the moment. With practice, the SEG mastered it. The method proved very popular and it wasn't long before both Princess Anne and Princess Margret were also happily employing the SEG on a routine basis.

Having mastered the technique of leapfrogging, it wasn't long before the concept of an 'easy-rider' became a necessity. The easy rider is a solo motorbike, which sits just a few yards ahead of the VIP vehicle. It maintains an easy pace, allowing the motorcycle escorts to leapfrog ahead with enough time to do their job safely. One officer recalled how the method came into practice:

'One of the royals – we won't mention names – had become a good customer of ours, a keen supporter of the group and extremely enthusiastic about our methods. We escorted this particular individual two or three times a week. The individual loved to travel at speed and would often call upon their driver to make more progress than was perhaps safe. The leapfroggers' legs weren't long enough to keep up! I ended up planting my car in front of the VIP vehicle (which the individual didn't like) to slow them down.'

To deter this sort of thing from happening in the future, and to help maintain timing, the SEG soon introduced the easy rider motorcyclist to all escorts. The method, albeit with significantly increased purpose, is still used today.

## New Kit, Training, Tasking and Control

After the motorcycles, the whistle is perhaps the most iconic and important piece of SEG equipment. It was introduced to the SEG by our very own PC Trevor Pryke. 'There had been complaints that British police were inefficient and occasionally impolite when stopping traffic, especially at busy junctions,' explained Trevor. The momentum of London's heavy traffic meant that police officers needed to take firm actions, often raising their voices to direct the flow. Trevor, however, was of the view that the majority of motorists would cooperate more readily if a calmer form of communication was used and he'd debated and discussed this with his teammate, PC Bob Caswell. Trevor had a simple idea: 'I took a whistle with me on an escort one day and used it – the result was staggering.'

Keen to see his idea put into action and become group policy, he organized a demonstration to senior officers. 'I met with a chief superintendent from the traffic division at the junction of Park Lane and Hyde Park Corner.' said Trevor. Together, they stood on the pavement of one of London's busiest intersections. 'I had boasted to him that from that position I could stop traffic in seconds. I put the mighty "thunderer" in my mouth and with a full lung of air I blew, calmly signalling drivers to stop by waving my hand.' The experiment had the desired result. 'To mine, and the chief superintendent's amazement, the traffic stopped. I blew again and waved them on, the traffic flowed at once.' Following Trevor's shrewd presentation, an order was issued that SEG officers were allowed to use whistles for directing traffic in London.

Trevor's whistle soon became an integral tool of the SEG. In future years, as the hum of London grew louder, and the sound of emergency vehicle sirens became ever more common, the SEG whistle was relied upon more and more. One retired officer recalled a member of the public asking him why his whistle was on a lanyard attached to his jacket. Surely he didn't think it was going to get stolen? 'No Sir, it's not for thieves,' responded the officer. 'It's so the doctor can pull the whistle out from my throat if I happen to swallow it!'

The whistle cuts through and above all other sounds and grabs attention. And, like a voice, it can be played to deliver a range of effects. As an escort leapfrogs ahead to the next junction, they might use a gentle double 'pip' to catch the attention of a motorist, or a long calm blow to sound the warning of an incoming convoy. A firm short blast commands your total and immediate attention. A flexible instrument, which can be played accordingly to the situation at hand, the whistle remains in use to this day despite the advances in siren technology.

I suspect that very few people across the policing community are aware that the SEG introduced the vehicle-mounted siren to the Metropolitan Police. Its impact on policing is extremely important and its song has become a familiar part of London's every day hum. This is the story.

Having been encouraged to join the team by PC Trevor Pryke, it emerged that PC Steve Brownridge was to share his eye for innovation. PC Brownridge (who later became a senior bodyguard in Royalty Protection) explained how, in the summer of 1979, the siren first came to the attention of the SEG:

'We were doing a pick up on the A3, where Hampshire officers were coming from Parkhurst [Prison in the Isle of Wight] to deliver a particular bad guy to Brixton Prison. They had a convoy of four vehicles, and rather than taking the convoy off them (which was normal practice) we decided to lead them to Brixton. What we didn't know was that they had a method for parting waves through the traffic. They had sirens – a noise we hadn't heard in London, only in films from America'.

The different sounds that we take for granted now were world stopping then. 'Everyone just stood and gasped; cars aimed for the hills, it was tremendous!' recalled Steve, 'I needed these. We needed these.' As soon as the convoy had stopped, PC Brownridge found himself searching under the bonnet of their cars to examine the sirens. They were made by Stirling Automotive in Essex. He made contact with the company and ordered several to test them on his own police vehicles.

The next challenge was to get approval to use the sirens from the senior ranks at New Scotland Yard. Initially this was easy as Commander Roger Croome gave his approval immediately. 'It wasn't long before we used the new system on convoys,' said Steve. 'It was life changing; it made a lovely noise. I actually made three lovely noises, the "yelp", the "wail" and the "two tone". It also featured a PA system. What an incredible bit of kit.' However, Commissioner David McNee then requested to hear the siren himself. 'He ordered it to be demonstrated to him in the basement at Lambeth HQ,' added Steve. 'We are talking underground carpark here. If ever there was a place not to use a siren this was it! It blew his ears out and he ordered that the wail function be banned.' Despite this setback, PC Brownridge soon convinced his superiors of the benefits of the wail feature and the SEG was given special permission to use it.

Thanks to Steve Brownridge and his initiative, and willingness to push forward, the siren was soon fitted to all sorts of other police vehicles across the Metropolitan Police.

With a number of IRA prison runs under their belts, it wasn't long before PC Brownridge, and a number of his colleagues in the SEG decided that they needed to include a different sort of vehicle into the fold. 'It became apparent that the rear vehicle should contain an officer looking rearwards all the time, with his weapon at the ready,' he said. 'To do this in a saloon car is impossible. I had a good relationship with the engineers at the Main Report Depot (MRD) and was aware that a Range Rover from the Bomb Squad was not being used to its full potential.' The vehicle was soon reallocated to the SEG to Steve's delight:

'After a few visits to MRD we ended up with a converted vehicle which had one large self-opening rear tail gate and a single swivelling seat facing rearwards with all sorts of weaponry and kit. The Rover also had searchlights attached to the roof as well as an illuminated "keep back" sign in the rear window which we had specially made – the first of its kind in the Metropolitan Police.'

The Range Rover proved to be a great vehicle for different types of escorts and continues to be used in an entirely new and updated format to this day.

During the 1950s and 1960s, training had played an important part of life in the SEG. However, with the increase in work came a reduction of time. Finding hours to give to dedicated practice proved difficult, although it was a necessity. Most training was on the job, with the more experienced officers acting as mentors for newer recruits. This system worked well at maintaining the status quo but was insufficient for practising new routines. It was time for a new security-focused training regime.

'Despite the extra workload, the precision team remained active, delivering between twenty to twenty-five displays a year on weekends,' explained Superintendent Johnson. Nearly all precision team training days took place in April, just ahead of the display season. During the mid to late 1970s, about half of the SEG was involved with the public displays. Lessons from the precision team trickled across into live escorts, which helped keep motorcycle skills sharp.

Some training though just couldn't be taught on the job. In light of the new security environment, it became obvious that arming the SEG was a justified and sensible move. However, the arming of officers required an entirely new set of operating procedures, operational tradecraft, and, of course, training. 'Firearms training', said Superintendent Johnson 'was delivered by the specialist firearms department, known as D11 internally to the police (later to become SO19).' D11 was to influence the development of the group's routines. Initially SEG was armed with Smith & Wesson guns with a 3 inch barrel. The guns had to be small as they were always concealed so as not to alarm the public, many of whom disagreed with the police being armed.

Working closely with D11, the SEG developed tactics for the use of firearms in the event of an attack. Many different scenarios were explored and acted out, including convoy manoeuvres, counter hijacks as well as escape and evasion driving. At the same time, different ways to improve SEG vehicles were being identified. For example, as one officer explained: 'In the event of an attack, it can be helpful to keep the windows open on the cars. For obvious reasons, in rainy weather, or when travelling at speed, this can be problematic.' A transparent plastic wind and rain deflector was specially adapted to be attached to all SEG vehicles – the first of its kind on police vehicles anywhere in the world. This sort of ingenuity, typical of the SEG, runs like a thick gold thread through its history.

SEG training days have always provided a safe place to test out new ideas and challenge the status quo. But then the history of policing is one sprinkled with examples of problem solving and creativity. Necessity is the mother of invention and, in certain circumstances inadequate finance, equipment and technology can positively challenge the mind. Couple this with a healthy culture of self-criticism, professional drive and determination, a good dose of humour, and an important charge and great ideas are born. The individuals who formed the SEG, together with their colleagues at the MRD, have demonstrated exceptional ingenuity over the years.

During the 1950s and 1960s, requests for SEG escorts usually came either from a senior officer within Traffic Division or from the ceremonials office at Canon Row Police Station. All requests were handled personally by John Baldwin. Although John belonged to Traffic Division during his time in the lead saddle, he'd been granted a great deal of independence from the normal chain of command, meaning that he had multiple bosses across the Metropolitan Police depending on the job at hand.

By the late 1970s, little had changed. Although the majority of the officers who made up the escorts officially belonged to Traffic Division, once on loan to the group, their line of command stopped with the inspector in charge of SEG. 'None of our duties came from our own line of command,' explained Superintendent Johnson. 'As a result, I was always heading over to New Scotland Yard, so as to keep my commander informed of what was going on.' Requests for SEG's support were coming in from all directions. With the widening of the group's mandate, other departments were now able to task them.

In a bold attempt to formalize what had become an overwhelming number of requests, a paper-flow route was established through the operations department of the Metropolitan Police, known internally as A8. All government departments could request the group's support through this channel. Most requests came from Special Branch, D11 (Prisons), A-Division Ceremonials, Prison and Specialist Firearms, and Government Hospitality (a part of the Foreign Office) for the movement of high-risk visiting dignitaries. 'Requests for royal escorts came to us direct from the Lord Chamberlain's office,' said Johnson. 'I would get requests for timings for royal routes either for our royal family or visiting royals. This included state visits.'

As more departments became aware of SEG's availability, the range of requests grew. Some were sensible and others not so. 'Letters and phone calls would come in from military officers, ambassadors, various police departments, senior government officials, staff of the royal household, even the BBC's then popular *Jim'll Fix it*', added a retired SEG officer. For the first time in history, the group was being challenged to keep up with demand, although it was a challenge that was welcomed with open arms.

## EL AL Aircrew Attack

On 20 August 1978, a Palestinian terrorist group attacked a private bus in central London, targeting crew members of the Israeli airline EL AL.

Twenty-one crew were onboard the bus. An air hostess was shot dead and a group of eight individuals, comprising crew and bystanders, were seriously injured. A taxi driver was blown from his cab by the blast wave from a grenade. One of the terrorists was also killed, dying of injuries caused by shrapnel ricochet from a grenade he'd thrown at the bus. A second terrorist was arrested at the scene by armed police. The third member of the terrorist group escaped. The ambush had taken place just as the crew's coach pulled up outside the Europa Hotel in Mayfair.

This wasn't the first attack against the Israeli air company. In 1968, flight EL AL 426 departed from London Heathrow destined for Israel via Italy. Before reaching its destination, the aircraft was hijacked by three Palestinian terrorists from the group Popular Front for the Liberation of Palestine (PFLP). The hijacking triggered a wave of attacks against EL AL and this same group claimed responsibility for the attack outside the Europa Hotel.

Following the attack, Israeli government officials were quick to criticize, demanding that security should have been provided for the aircrew. They also accused the UK of a lack of urgency when tackling Palestinian terrorism. Their criticism and demands struck at the very heart of government, and their wishes were met through a series of decisive actions.

During the late 1960s and early 1970s, the UK's security response to Palestinian terrorism had been limited. In his book *The Defence of the Realm (the Authorized History of MI5)*, Christopher Andrew wrote:

'The first PFLP attacks on Jewish targets in London were so amateurish that they had failed to give a greater sense of urgency to British counter terrorism. Incendiary devices planted in Oxford Street at Selfridges and Marks and Spencer on 18th July 1969 caused minimal damage. A third PFLP bomb attack, not far away at the Israeli Zim Shipping Office in Regent Street, was slightly more successful, breaking several windows and causing minor injuries.'

The rise in terrorism generally and, in particular, the PFLP's proven capacity to deliver attacks within Europe, forced the British security to adapt, and as a consequence, alterations to its counter terrorism strategy were made. Two of the most noteworthy alterations were to the security architecture itself, with the formation of the Special Air Service (SAS) Counter Terrorist unit, as well as a significant increase in funding and mandate for the specialist police teams belonging to the Metropolitan Police, especially Special Branch, Royalty Protection Group and the SEG.

With the changes came an increased need for a working partnership with Special Branch, other specialist police teams, the SAS and the SEG. But relationships like these aren't made overnight. They take months to mature. As relationships built and joint working practices flourished, each of the specialist teams benefited from the other's experience. As a combined workforce, the SEG was now at the helm of a strong multiagency protection team. A deterrent by nature, preventative and peaceful by preference, fierce if needed.

As a consequence of the newly-acquired mission to provide high security escorts, the relationship between the SEG and Special Branch grew particularly close. One retired SEG officer recalled an episode that illustrates how fond the two departments become of each other:

'To help with our professional working relationship, we'd started to socialise together with officers from Special Branch. The chief superintendent occasionally attended these events. He was known to roll his own cigarettes, keeping his tobacco in a simple Golden Virginia tin box. In the absence of his knowledge, said tin box was temporarily 'removed' from the chief super's possession. One of my colleagues had it chrome plated and inscribed 'SEG' before presenting the more appropriately dressed box to its owner.'

The relationship was to only get stronger.

'The attack against the EL AL aircrew changed everything for the SEG,' explained Superintendent Johnson. Within days the group had received orders to provide armed escorts to all further EL AL crew for movements between the airport and their hotels. Despite advice from the British security agencies 'the air crew refused to move to a hotel nearer to the airport,' added Johnson. 'We were tasked to provide escorts for each flight departure and arrival. This committed at least two cars every day for the following two years.' Any concerns about returning to the group's part-time existence were over. From this period on, authorization was given that all further SEG runs would be armed.

## The Funeral of Lord Mountbatten

Admiral of the Fleet 1st Earl Mountbatten of Burma, known informally as Lord Mountbatten of Burma (aged 79), together with his grandson Nicholas (aged 14), his daughter's mother in law, Doreen, Lady Brabourne (aged 83) and a member of staff – the boat boy, Paul (aged 15) – were assassinated in an explosion whilst cruising in a private leisure boat. Also aboard the boat was his eldest daughter Patricia, her husband John, and his second grandson who survived but suffered serious injuries.

Lord Mountbatten was heralded as one of the greatest statesmen and naval officers in British history. He was the last British viceroy of India following their independence in 1947. An uncle of Prince Philip, and a cousin of HMQ, he had served as Supreme Allied Commander during the Second World War. Following the war, he took up the position of First Sea Lord, thereafter becoming Chief of the Defence Staff until 1965, making him the longest-serving head of the British Armed Forces to date. He was a majestic war hero, beloved by British people and a target of the IRA.

1952. The founding group of SEG officers being inspected at Hendon Police College shortly after their first set of rehearsals for the visit of Marshall Tito. (© *Mayor's Office of Policing and Crime*)

A motorcycle escort leapfrogging at pace towards a busy junction.

Bikes in the Royal
Mews ready for
another state visit.

Bikes lined up during
the Pope's visit to the
UK in 1982.

Current times. The
tradition of precise
display continues.

EL AL crew delivered safely to the aircraft, 1978.

EMPÉROR HIROHITO
1971

Emperor Hirohito inspecting the SEG at the end of his visit 1971. (© *Mayor's Office of Policing and Crime*)

Friend and colleague of the SEG, Martyn Hillier of Gloucestershire Police outside 10 Downing Street.

Happy to be in the SEG. Eugenie Brooks with her trusty BMW motorcycle.

First man in space, Yuri Gagarin, together with his SEG escort. (© *Mayor's Office of Policing and Crime*)

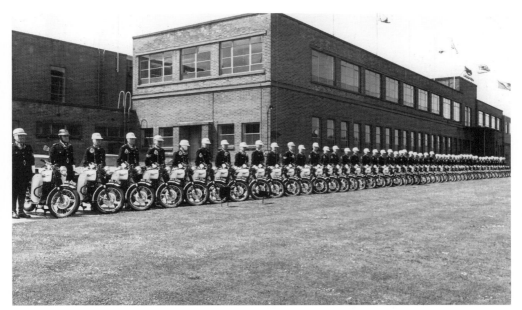

Met Police Traffic Contingent outside the Triumph Meriden factory en-route to the investiture of HRH Prince of Wales at Caernarfon.

Inspector John Gouldsmith, Head of the SEG, Sergeant John Swain, and Princess Diana following an SEG go-kart charity event. (© *Mayor's Office of Policing and Crime*)

B.6/8

## METROPOLITAN POLICE
### MOTOR DRIVING SCHOOL REPORT
#### RECLASSIFICATION COURSE
#### ADVANCED CAR _____ WING

NAME __PRYKE__    RANK __P.C.__    DIVISION __'S'__ Dt.6

DIVL. No. __250__    WARRANT No. __143780__    AGE __27__ _____ YEARS

DUTY ON WHICH EMPLOYED __Ordinary Duty__

COURSE No. __185__    PERIOD from __24.2.65__   to: __9.3.65__

PERCENTAGE OF MARKS OBTAINED FOR:-

| TRAFFIC LAW | PRACTICAL MAINTENANCE | DRIVING RIDING | ROADCRAFT AND HIGHWAY CODE | PLANS |
|---|---|---|---|---|
| | | 90 | 88 | |
| GENERAL KNOWLEDGE | MECHANICAL THEORY | TYRE CHANGING | OBSTACLES REVERSING | SKIDDING |
| | | | | 92 |

* RESULT:- Passed or Failed    __Passed__

* Driving Classification    __I__

Remarks

P.C. Pryke worked very hard whilst on the course and
has developed into quite a good driver. He is systematic
and brisk with quite a good pattern. Now needs to acquire
a little more polish. Has the ability to maintain a high
standard. He became the best student on the course.

DATE __10.3.65__      (Sgd.) R. R. Reynolds
                         Chief Supt., B.8.

         Drives to a good pattern

DATE __11.3.65__      (Sgd.) D. C. Macdonald
                         Deputy Commander 'B'.

---

B.6/8

## METROPOLITAN POLICE
### MOTOR DRIVING SCHOOL REPORT
#### ADVANCED MOTOR CYCLE _____ WING

NAME __PRYKE__    RANK __P.C.__    DIVISION __'S'__

DIVL. No. __250__    WARRANT No. __143780__    AGE __25__ _____ YEARS

DUTY ON WHICH EMPLOYED __TRAFFIC PATROL__

COURSE No. __185__    PERIOD from __3.12.62__   to __22.12.62__

PERCENTAGE OF MARKS OBTAINED FOR:-

| TRAFFIC LAW | PRACTICAL MAINTENANCE | DRIVING RIDING | ROADCRAFT AND HIGHWAY CODE | PLANS |
|---|---|---|---|---|
| | 93 | 90 | 75 | |
| GENERAL KNOWLEDGE | MECHANICAL THEORY | TYRE CHANGING | OBSTACLES REVERSING | SKIDDING |
| | 97 | | | |

* RESULT:- Passed or Failed    __PASSED__

* Driving Classification    __CLASS 1__

Remarks

P.C. Pryke has developed into a safe brisk competent
rider, but must ensure that he always makes an early and
correct assessment of hazards.

DATE __27.12.62.__      (Sgd) R. R. Reynolds
                          Chief Supt., B.8.

         Satisfactory

DATE __28.12.62__      (Sgd) N. Radford.
                         Deputy Commander (Transport)

Copies to:-

PC Trevor Pryke passes his Advanced Car and Motorcycle courses

BUCKINGHAM PALACE

6th June, 1986.

Dear Constable Pryke,

I am commanded by The Queen to
thank you very much for the kind message
of loyal greetings which you have sent
on the occasion of your retirement from
the Metropolitan Police after thirty years
service.

Her Majesty greatly appreciated
your message, and sends her best wishes
for a long and happy retirement.

Yours sincerely,

Kenneth Scott

Police Constable Trevor Pryke.

NEW SCOTLAND YARD,
BROADWAY, LONDON, S.W.1

CRJW/HAL

26 July 1971

PC 887'TD' Pryke
TDQ

Dear Mr Pryke

You have participated recently in a display by the
Metropolitan Police at the Royal Agricultural Show
Stoneleigh, that will long be remembered with pride
by your associates in this Force and with delight
by the audiences as a whole.

I am very grateful for the enthusiasm of the Traffic
Division contingent, as exemplified by their outstanding
performance, and wish to express my personal
congratulations to you for your part in achieving this
success.

Yours sincerely

C P J Woods
Assistant Commissioner (Traffic)

A letter on behalf of the Queen to PC Trevor Pryke on the occasion of
his retirement.

Royal Show letter of thanks.

CLARENCE HOUSE
ST. JAMES'S

The Household Staff of
Her Majesty Queen Elizabeth The Queen Mother
request the pleasure of the company of

P.C. & Mrs Trevor Pryke

at a Reception at St. James's Palace on
Tuesday, 18th December, 1984

6.30-8 p.m.
(please bring this card with you)
Entrance by
Marlborough Road Door

R.S.V.P. The Steward,
Clarence House,
St. James's, S.W.1

SEG Officers are occasionally invited to attend private royal events.

President George Bush Snr sitting aloft an
SEG motorcycle outside Winfield House. Bush
is a huge fan of the SEG.

SEG Officer Trevor Pryke on the range.

Precision Team motorcycle after a collision during practice.

Rear gunner. The Range Rover was converted to hold a rear facing seat. Doors were opened via a foot pedal.

SEG Christmas card celebrating the life of Sir Winston Churchill.

'Of all the trains and all the crossings'.......

SEG Christmas card. Holding back a train for Her Majesty the Queen!

ON HER MAJESTY'S SECRET SERVICE

SEG Christmas card. Peter Skerrit as red diamond and John Gouldsmith making an excellent Santa.

SEG Christmas card. Rembering the Italian state visit. The Italian Job!

SEG Christmas card. Remembering the Traffic Patrol routes of the SEG.

10th April 2017. SEG turning at the funeral of PC Keith Palmer.

Sergeant John Swain, now retired, reunited with the SEG Range Rover he drove at Princess Diana's funeral.

Single motorcycle escort momentarily holding back traffic.

Steely horses ready for work.

The Popemobile. Drawn by a child for an art competition by the agency that designed the actual vehicle together with the SEG.

The two Princes and their mother, Princess Diana, in SEG uniforms at the 'Garage' in Barnes. (© *Mayor's Office of Policing and Crime*)

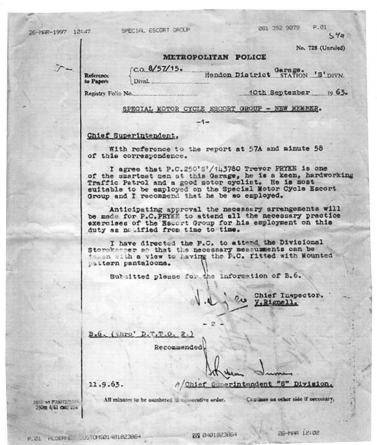

Trevor Pryke, recommendation to be posted by the SEG.

Two motorcycle escorts leading a royal vehicle towards Buckingham Palace.

Valentina Terishcova, first woman in space 1963, stood in the gardens of the Russian Embassy with John Baldwin and his team. (© *Mayor's Office of Policing and Crime*)

1985. SEG group photo at Hendon Police College. (© *Mayor's Office of Policing and Crime*)

No one could have imagined, or predicted the tragedies that would unfold on the gentle summer day of 27 August 1979. The explosion, which completely disintegrated the vessel, happened moments after the boat motored away from landfall. Lord Mountbatten had intended on spending a long summer break with his family at their home in Mullaghmore, County Sligo, on the north west coast of Ireland. The assassination took place in full view of his Garda police security team. In a catastrophic breach of security, a bomb had been placed under the floorboards of the boat during the darkness of the night. Just hours later, eighteen British army soldiers were killed and six seriously injured (more than in any other PIRA operation in the history of the Troubles) in an explosion at Warrenpoint. The IRA claimed responsibility for both attacks. The bombs were believed to be detonated by remote control.

Lord Mountbatten had been deeply involved in the planning of his state funeral. A great lover of pomp and ceremony, he'd hoped his funeral would be a moment of optimism for the British public. Months before his death, he famously said: 'I'm looking forward to my own funeral. It should be a great do and great fun.' However, due to the terrible nature of his death, the event carried an additionally heavy air of sadness.

Without hesitation, the SEG was given the great honour of escorting Lord Mountbatten's coffin from his home in Romsey, Hampshire, to London in preparation for the funeral service. As one retired officer recalled: 'The most emotional event of my career was bringing the body of Lord Mountbatten to lie in state at the chapel at St James's Palace.' The public weren't given any advance notice about the movement of the coffin. Despite this, the officer said 'the public reaction, when they saw the hearse surrounded by our motorcycle escort, the back-up car and the helicopter hovering above, was so dramatic, I don't think there was a single SEG officer with dry eyes. They immediately recognized the situation and stood to attention as we passed them by.'

As the escort progressed along the M3 towards London, a number of motorists overtook them. 'We were restricted to forty-five miles per hour, any faster and the hearse would look untidy,' explained Superintendent Johnson. 'Kenyon's, funeral directors to the royal family, had given us very clear instructions. I remember some of the motorists wearing caps, and removing them as they overtook us as a mark of respect,'

On 5 September 1979, tens of thousands of people lined the cortege route between St James's Palace and Westminster Abbey. Millions watched from their homes. The scale of the event, the attendance, and the overall public reaction to his death, is often likened to that of Winston Churchill's. After the funeral service, Lord Mountbatten's coffin was driven in an open back British Army Land Rover to Waterloo Station, where he was placed on a special train, accompanied by members of his own family, as well as the royals. Their final destination was the site of his burial, at his family home in Romsey.

The specially-converted Land Rover was escorted by a group of tanks, with the SEG at the front of the cortege. On this occasion the cortege travelled slowly, at an average of 5mph, a little above the average pedestrian walking pace. Although it may seem straightforward, riding at low speed, in a perfectly straight line, whilst maintaining a generally tidy look, requires a great deal of skill and practice. This is especially true when riding in a synchronized fashion with several other motorcycles. At normal traffic speeds, motorcycles are comparatively lightweight in relation to their power, making them nimble and nippy, but also easy to ride smoothly. However, at very low speeds, the full weight of the bike comes into play, making it hard to balance and resulting in a tendency to wobble.

Furthermore, if a motorcycle isn't tuned for low speed riding, the engine will generate too much or too little power for the speed, causing the rider to balance throttle, clutch and brake to keep a steady pace. 'At the time of Mountbatten's funeral, our mechanic at the SEG was a gentleman from Sri Lanka called Wickie,' explained Superintendent Johnson. 'He was excellent with the bikes. He tuned all of the bikes to run smoothly at low revs so we could slow ride more easily. Originally experienced with Triumphs, when we converted to BMWs he found his way around them very quickly, always adapting them perfectly to the needs of our duties.' The motorcycles performed to perfection as they escorted Mountbatten to Waterloo. Wickie's contribution had ensured the SEG once again fulfilled its role with the precision and elegance that such an event commanded. The mechanic, or position of 'garage hand', as it was later to become known, was one of the bedrocks of the group.

## The Show Must Go On – The 150th Anniversary of the Metropolitan Police

With the passing of the first Metropolitan Police Act in 1829, London's professional police force was created. One hundred and fifty years on, the anniversary celebrations provided a wonderful platform to show off some of the talent and capability of the world's finest police service. Numerous smaller events had been organized across the year, with the excitement culminating in a large tattoo show at Wembley Stadium between 12 and 17 October 1979. The show was a sell out, and on the night before the finale, HMQ chose to occupy the royal box and watch on eagerly.

Having returned temporarily to the group to help out for the occasion, Sergeant Jock Shields led the training at Imber Court – a police social club located in south-east London. In preparation for the big event, the MPT had doubled in size by bringing in class one advanced motorists from across London's traffic garages. A second team, comprised entirely of regular traffic officers, was led by Sergeant Boatwright and was ready to give a great show of cross overs, slow, fast and precision driving. Weeks of practice and rehearsal had brought the two teams close together. During training, some of the team had buddied up with officers from the Mounted Branch, who were also featuring in the anniversary show. 'In the late mornings and afternoons, Peter Roberts, Bob Caswell and myself would ride on their horses, and they would have a go on our bikes around the arena,' recalled PC Trevor Pryke. The sense of camaraderie between the two departments was strong as they had met and performed together before, most memorably at the Royal Agricultural Society's Royal Show.

Scores of police departments had been invited to participate, with each providing its own unique display of talent to entertain the crowds. The MPT had initially been given a seventeen-minute time slot, but a few weeks prior to the show this was reduced to just ten minutes, due to a change in the schedule. The dimensions of the stadium were also much smaller – and a different shape – from what the team were used to. The knock-on effect meant the team had to think on its feet and make a large number of adjustments to the normal routine.

However, a reduction in time wasn't the only surprise in store for them. 'When we arrived at the stadium, the floor was covered in peat,' recalled one former officer. 'We discovered the stadium had just been used for the annual horse show. Our first rehearsal was pretty traumatic. The bikes were fitted with road tyres, making it nearly impossible to stay upright on the dry loose surface.' Following a discussion with the organizers, they agreed to change the surface. 'The following morning we arrived to see a tractor pouring a deep layer of condensed soil across the stadium floor,' he added. 'The new surface was much better suited to our bikes and was also suitable for the Mounted Branch. With a bit of careful practice, we managed to make it alright on the night.'

As the curtain lifted, a group of twenty motorcyclists and a single police vehicle entered in arrow formation coming to rest in the centre of the arena. Superintendent Rick Johnson, leader of the SEG, stepped out from the passenger seat of the car, stood to attention, and gave a salute. Ten of the bikes then drove away from the formation, circling the edge of the arena before disappearing out of sight. The remaining ten then began their display of precision riding. The audience was suitably wowed. Shortly after the show, Trevor sent HMQ a telegram thanking her for attending the event. She responded with her own telegram thanking them for a wonderful display. The MPT was, without any question of doubt, the jewel in the crown of the show.

## 'We Lead Others Follow' – The Coat of Arms

The process of 'route n' a run (or recce) had been crucial practice prior to any new escort since the mid 1960s. It allowed officers to time routes from A-Z, observe road conditions, and assess traffic flows at certain times of day. Occasionally they'd also use the opportunity to meet with personnel at the collection and drop-off points, put faces to names and talk over the finer details of protocol, which was especially helpful for high-profile runs.

Returning from one such recce, riding along the M40 side by side with PC Bob Caswell, PC Trevor Pryke remembered 'seeing a sign on the back of a removal lorry which said "We Lead Others Follow". Tapping Bob on his shoulder, I said "that should be the motto of the SEG!"' Back at the garage, the suggestion was well received and the idea spread quickly through the grapevine to other police departments. Some weeks later, while sitting having dinner in a police canteen, a Wembley Garage traffic officer by the name of Ian Mackenzie came over to Trevor and offered to make a coat of arms for the group. 'His hobby was heraldry,' explained Trevor. 'For the princely sum of £25, I received the first ever production.'

Some years later the coat of arms was submitted to the College of Arms for their inspection. Although not an official coat of arms, the college said the 'method and style of the crest met the professional heraldic standards held by the college itself.' Thanks to PC John Swain (retired), in March 2016 the crest received its own 'certificate of registration of design' from the Designs and Trade Marks Intellectual Property Office.

The description of the crest is as follows: the royal crown and helmet are from the original Metropolitan Police coat of arms. The white fretwork represents the cross overs performed by the MPT. The white spots represent a diamond formation performed by escorts on the road's black tarmac. The VIP car is purple, which is the original call sign for HMQ, and the car leaves a golden wake to signify royalty.

**Triumph TR6 Trophy – Saint (1967–1980 approx).** Fondly known in police circles as the 'Saint' (Stop Anything In No Time), the TR6 was based on the Thunderbird but contained numerous upgrades, most noteworthy of which was the new twin leading shoe front brake. Since the motorcycle didn't have panniers, wet weather gear would be neatly folded and strapped to the top of the fuel tank. A nimble and easily manoeuvred bike at slow speed, the Trophy was extremely popular with traffic police officers. Indeed, the TR6 was so popular with the police across the UK that a factory was opened dedicated to the production of bespoke police motorcycles, known as the TR6P. Over the years the SEG made several alterations, including the addition of white plastic leg shields and protective polished steel crash bars.

# The 1980s

## News Bikes and a New Home

The south was booming as pin-striped yuppies drove go-fast Quattros and boogied on to Billy Ocean. London was celebrating the 'Loadsamoney' era of a flourishing economy. Elsewhere, miners marched with boots striking the ground as our first female prime minister presided over a period of privatization. Shifting economic models created friction up and down the country.

The SEG had something to celebrate. Now with a garage of its own, located in the prestigious inner London suburb of Barnes, 2 January 1980 saw SEG finally established as a permanent team. It had taken nearly three decades but it was well worth the wait. The group's incredible legacy had provided strong foundations on which to build. Respected by the highest echelons across government, trusted by the royal household, and admired by colleagues across the police, the SEG was to be well supported by its superiors in traffic division.

The new garage was located on Barnes High Street, within a collection of exclusive shops, bars, restaurants and pubs, and adjacent to the River Thames. 'We took over about a third of the building', explained Superintendent Johnson. 'In addition to the operational teams, we had an office manager, a storeman/armourer, and even an administrative clerk.' The group had also taken receipt of a fleet of brand new top of the range BMW R80 motorcycles. Despite the group's long history with Triumph, it was time for a change.

Although the Triumphs had been extremely popular, the BMWs were far superior bikes. Everyone agreed. 'The Triumphs were beautiful, packed with personality and charm, but they were loud, rattled and vibrated, and often leaked oil,' admitted one retired officer. The new bikes were smoother, more reliable, much more powerful and stopped more quickly. They were customized for the job, as PC Bob Stewart explained: 'When you are manoeuvring through traffic you've got to be able to see your front wheel. With fairing fitted you can't, so we had the engineers remove the front and upper parts of it, leaving leg protection only.'

The new garage meant the whole team was under one roof for the first time since its formation, having previously operated out of several traffic garages across London. Morale was already good but sharing one space increased the group's cohesion and sense of unity even more. 'Since I had all of the men in one place, I'd split them up from their old garage teams and mixed them into new ones,' said Johnson. 'It worked well and everyone got on tremendously. They formed an impressive unit.' Jokes and banter were encouraged and not even Superintendent Johnson was above getting involved with the pranks:

'Privately, I'd bought a new Honda motorcycle, which I used to get to and from work. The dealer had given me a book of 'Honda' stickers. As a joke, I put some of these stickers on the privately-owned BMW motorcycles belonging to some of the PCs. I went into my office one morning and found my motorcycle sitting on my desk! It remained there, two floors up from the garage, until they took pity on me, and helped me take it back downstairs.'

With the SEG's impressive history and a twenty-year anniversary just around the corner, the new home helped make it feel established and no longer out on a limb. Although the SEG's work will always be far from mainstream police business, the new permanence was accompanied by a welcomed sense of normality; a wall on which to hang a picture or mount a coat of arms; a staffroom in which to sit, chat and joke with colleagues; a locker in which to place boot polish and hang a helmet. SEG now had a private space in which to stamp its identity.

As the group rolled on, the workload began to snowball and it amassed an increasingly-diverse range of customers, including politicians, heads of government departments and priceless works of art and gold. The list goes on. As one retired SEG officer said: 'If you couldn't insure it, we'd escort it.' Many days would see overlapping escorts, and some SEG officers were involved in more than one run a day.

The 1980s were to have violent beginnings and the turmoil would last throughout the decade. It was a continuation from the 1970s when British security agencies had to deal with the attempted kidnap of HRH Princess Anne, and the assassination of Lord Mountbatten amongst other events. In May 1981, the IRA failed in its attempt to kill HMQ during her visit to a British Petroleum (BP) oil terminal in the Shetland Islands. Many thought the situation couldn't get any worse, but it did. A full-scale tri-service war with Argentina and a relentless campaign of IRA bombs, embassy sieges, and international terrorist groups on the increase meant a busy decade lay ahead.

'During the early '80s international terrorists, against whom the security service retained the lead intelligence role, mounted considerably more attacks in mainland Britain than the IRA,' wrote Christopher Andrew in *The Defence of the Realm*. 'Unlike IRA operations, international terrorist attacks were usually spill-overs from conflicts in other parts of the world, mainly in the Middle East, and rarely targeted British interests directly.' That said, many of the foreign dignitaries and world leaders protected by the SEG were attractive target for such terrorist groups. 'Security was once again at the top of our agenda,' explained one former SEG officer.

A diary note from a retired SEG officer summed up the current climate, and the group's responses rather well:

'In the past few years, the Police Service has become more aware of the importance of transferring High Security or High Risk personnel from one location to another as quickly as possible. The problems faced by European countries have not reached us to the same extent, but already we are getting increasing terrorist incidents, which are making people more aware of the need for better training and equipment. During the last few years the SEG have become more involved in high security movements, whilst still trying to keep the traditional police image, but the traditional image should not be kept to the exclusion of efficiency.'

Observant of attacks during the 1970s, and conscious of the threats that lay ahead, SEG was primed, poised and prepared to take on whatever the decade had in store. In the words of 1980s pop star Billy Ocean: 'When the going gets tough, the tough get going!'

The British security community had been forced to adapt and respond to ever-increasing and changing demands. Contingency planning, training and rehearsing became more sophisticated and had to consider a greater range of scenarios. Just four months into the decade, in April 1980, almost every department in London's counter-terrorist community was to be put to the test in a security incident unlike any that had been experienced before.

## Selecting the Best

By the early 1980s, the requirements needed to become an SEG officer were well established. It was essential that standards were kept high. In addition to holding each of the advanced driving certificates, both for motorcycle and car, applicants were expected to have passed with a top score. Furthermore, in addition to having several years' experience of normal police driving, an applicant should have also demonstrated their advanced skills for a minimum of two to three years before applying for the group.

Applicants also needed the full support and recommendation of their supervisor. Although individuals were welcome to apply, in reality, many officers were nominated by their superiors, normally due to exemplary performance. Personal character references would be thoroughly examined and questioned. Due to a high volume of applicants, and only a small number of positions, it was relatively easy to ensure that successful applicants were well suited to the job. They were of a similar standard and of a similar mindset. Joking about the work culture at the SEG, one retired officer said: 'One inspector, two sergeants, and thirty-two superintendents – the escorts! The SEG is no place for anyone who struggles with leadership and initiative.'

Prior to joining the group, officers would undergo rigorous firearms training. Once in the group, the newly-appointed team member would spend several months with an experienced officer, who, in turn, would provide mentoring and advice. 'To keep everyone as sharp as possible, whenever time permitted, we'd request or organize our own training day for SEG officers who had been serving with the group for some time,' explained one retired officer. 'Two of the lads went away to qualify as physical training instructors for just such occasions.'

The enormity and wide-ranging responsibility of a SEG officer's job meant every single group member had to be trained and prepared for almost any scenario. As this 1982 diary entry from the hand of a retired SEG officer explained:

'The SEG have traditionally been used as escorts for pomp and ceremony. All officers have always had to be advanced motor car [drivers] and motor cyclists, now they have to undergo firearms training to an advanced level, which includes training with vehicles whilst in a convoy situation. We're beginning to develop our own courses, including counter hijack, together with other specialist departments, including the military. We're also starting to learn how to drive unusual vehicles, including passenger coaches, 4x4s in off-road conditions, and other emergency vehicles. The security threats are considerable, and we must train for all possibilities.'

It was a winter's day in late 1985 and I was 6 years old. While searching for a VHS recording of that summer's Live Aid concert (which had been the first time I'd heard the majestic band Queen), I discovered a VHS tape resting on my dad's desk, marked 'counter hijack course'. Together with one of my older brothers, we took the enticingly-sounding video, placed it inside the video recorder and started to watch what seemed to us like a Hollywood action movie – only this film starred my father. Set in what was presumably a private airfield somewhere just outside of London, it opened with a distant shot of my father and a number of his colleagues sitting on white, plastic chairs by the side of the airstrip. They were holding mugs, drinking tea and enjoying what very much looked like Rich Tea biscuits and doughnuts. Impatiently, we fast forwarded the video, only pausing once the cameraman was clearly sitting inside a police vehicle.

'Go! Go! Go!' boomed the man in the passenger seat. You could only see familiar eyes in the rear-view mirror, a small part of his arm, hands connecting to the gear level and a well-worn steering wheel. I immediately noticed how he clutched the gear lever. It was so different. Rather than cupping his hand over the top of the lever, he gripped it by the side, placing his thumb on the top. Depending on which gear he selected, his hand would change position, sometimes reversing the position so his thumb was at the bottom or wrapped around the lever. I later discovered this technique helps the driver select the correct gear quickly at high speed, or in action situations. The car was now in reverse and increasing speed. I could see the red and white traffic cones (which were spaced equally apart about double the width of the car) disappear as we catapulted backwards. The speedo was now recording 40mph. Suddenly, with a controlled turn of the steering wheel the car spun a full 180 degrees. Now gently rolling, but facing forward, and still perfectly positioned between the cones, the car powered on.

The video continued. My brother and I were now off the sofa and sitting on the carpet directly under the television. It was time to get down to brass tacks. Our driver, who was now seated in a rather scruffy Jaguar, was ready to go. The cones had gone, but ahead on the tarmac we could see two cars parked nose-to-nose and side on to the Jaguar – it was a road block. 'When it's not possible to reverse out of this situation, you must ram as fast as possible,' announced the instructor. 'Hit where the noses of the cars meet, and maintain power on impact.' I turned to my brother. 'Wow. Is this really happening?' I asked. He looked at me with a beaming smile. 'I think so, Chris. I think so.' As the engine roared into action, the bonnet of the Jaguar lifted. Seconds later we'd made impact. Both of the parked cars were thrown to the side, spinning out, and creating an opening for the Jaguar to pass through. Surprisingly there appeared to be very little damage on 'our' vehicle.

We saw J-turns, U-turns, high-speed reversing, skid-pan sliding, pursuit driving and more. At one point even the front windscreen was blacked out with a blanket to replicate paint being thrown, or a smashed windscreen. The driver had to continue performing the manoeuvres but with very limited vision. The video was one whole action movie with driver after driver repeating the death-defying stunts until they were perfected. It was great fun for us viewers. But what was it like to take part? 'At first it's very exciting but as a student you quickly realize that the instructors aren't there for your entertainment,' explained one retired officer. 'They make the training as realistic as possible, and albeit everything is done in good humour, they take their work very seriously, and expect students to reach high standards quickly.'

Several years later, my father organized for me to attend a couple of days training on what was then called the national bodyguards' course. The first part of the training took place in a classroom at Hendon Police College packed with police officers from all over the UK. Our instructor, PC Peter Skerritt, my chaperone and an experienced SEG member, began his lecture with the words: 'Early vision means an early decision. Look, think and plan ahead.' One of the primary skills of an advanced police driver is to scan the horizon, looking ahead, to the side and behind for potential hazards. It may sound easy, but I have since found out that it's a difficult skill to acquire, and even more challenging to put into practice. The key is to practise through repetition, repetition, and even more repetition. 'You're here today because we want you to become thinking drivers,' continued the instructor. The hours that followed were full of tips, techniques, and diagrams of road traffic scenarios. Students offered ideas and answers. A little bored of the chalk and talk, I was looking forward to seeing all that we'd learnt be put into practice.

With the sound of sirens wailing in the background, our instructor began to speak: 'We're approaching roundabout in twenty metres, green coach ahead indicating left, blue Escort approaching second entrance of roundabout, check mirrors, heavy goods vehicle to rear, slow to second gear, pedestrian looking to cross the road at mouth of roundabout, prepare to stop, keep rolling, mirrors, clear and move ahead.' The commentary had been spoken to the student, who was sitting attentively in the passenger seat of the SEG Rover Saloon. I was in the rear of the car taking it all in. I remember thinking how remarkably calm PC Skerritt was as we drove speedily along the busy street. His observation skills and ability to describe the surrounding environment were incredible. Window open, we pulled into the roundabout. Peter put his arm out of the driver's window and offered a quick smile, thank you and wave to the driver of the blue Escort he'd stopped just moments before.

The commentary was continuous as we progressed across central London, occasionally driving through red lights and sometimes manoeuvring into the other side of the road, controlling oncoming traffic as we did. Although we reached high speeds in densely-populated streets, I had total confidence that the public were always kept safe. PC Skerritt had complete control over the car and his situational awareness of the surrounding hazards appeared faultless. As we reached our destination, some forty-five minutes after departure, I remember feeling mentally drained. The student made remarks of a similar nature. Peter however seemed to be in top shape, and ready to take on his next student, who stood patiently by the side of the kerb.

The driving style Peter had demonstrated was as much about car control as it was about a particular sort of mindset. Teaching someone to drive quickly is usually rather straightforward and can be achieved through repetition, increasing speed on each training run. The thinking part though can be more challenging. The 'commentary', as it is known in police circles, is an important part of learning to drive safely at speed, especially through congested areas. It's taught to all Advanced and Emergency Response drivers in the police. The commentary itself involves the driver searching his or her environs, both near and far, and then speaking out loud to acknowledge potential hazards. Speaking out loud helps the student develop the skills more quickly and allows the instructor to measure progress. At first, the process of narrating a commentary can be exhausting. Drivers tend to get tongue-tied and speak too slowly or too quickly. It can even affect their driving, causing them to adjust their speed irrationally. Often, at first, they will say too much or too little. Learning to focus on the priorities comes with experience. Eventually though, with much practice, the process becomes a habit. No longer will the driver need to speak out, and searching for hazards becomes instinctive, automatic and effortless.

Normally the police drivers who employ commentary thinking are driving in a single vehicle, often responding to some sort of emergency call. For the SEG, the commentary is far more complex. By their very nature, escorts involve multiple vehicles, so additional concentration is needed to keep the convoy together in busy traffic. With increased numbers of convoy vehicles there are of course increased hazards. Additionally, horizon-scanning for the SEG must include the identification of potential violent threats, not just vehicle or pedestrian safety hazards. This is complicated by the fact motorcycle escorts leap forward at speed to control junctions. And all this happens while keeping the VIP vehicle rolling at a steady and calm speed, and arriving at the destination at exactly the right time.

High selection standards, thorough training, perfectly precise procedures and cutting edge equipment may provide a strong foundation for good results, but it is not infallible. In spite of all these elements, there are many examples of teams failing to work properly. Sometimes it's because they lack urgency in their purpose or are weak in communication. They might rebuff inclusiveness or struggle with leadership. Without the creativity to overcome the uncongenial, many teams lack the confidence to embrace humour and playfulness in their work. They might even be deficient in *esprit de corps*.

The SEG has, and always has had, an abundance of the above. A strong sense of purpose and a willingness to learn from each run (the 'post mortem') create a tough team, resilient to knocks with a professionalism second to none outside the military.

## Iranian Embassy Siege

Heart-racing adrenaline, intense fear, anger, outrage, focus, determination and possibly even excitement – it's all a matter of perspective, depending on the part you played. The show that followed over the six-day siege was dramatic from all points of view.

On 30 April 1980, six heavily-armed Iranian terrorists successfully infiltrated security at the Iranian Embassy in London. Within minutes they'd taken twenty-six hostages who were a mixture of embassy staff and members of the public. Confident and unrelenting, they made their demands known. First they wanted the release of Arab prisoners in Khuzestan and then they wanted a safe passage out of the UK. The entire saga unfolded in view of the world's media and general public as millions watched on their TVs. It came six days after the US had attempted a rescue mission in Iran. Their aim was to release fifty-two US Embassy staff who'd been taken hostage, but the mission failed and was aborted midway. A hostage-taking of this kind was a first in the UK. Through the police negotiator, the British government relayed the decision that safe passage would not be granted at this stage. A six-day siege ensued, during which time the British security community was brought together to manage what was a new problem for the UK.

The Metropolitan Police was in charge and a large number of police officers were already at the scene. However, with a seemingly limited range of options, a back-up plan was needed. The government called in the SAS, requesting the attendance of the recently-formed and relatively-untested counter-terrorist unit. The SAS began the process of forming an 'immediate action' (IA) plan. IA plans are used if a worst-case scenario begins to unfold, such as if the terrorists began to kill hostages. The embassy itself is a terraced townhouse, located at 16 Princess Gate, in the diplomatic quarter of South Kensington. On arrival at the scene, the SAS took control of the buildings attached either side of the embassy and began to form a plan of attack.

'What happened that day formed one of my most memorable experiences during my police service,' said a retired SEG officer. 'I was sitting watching the news on TV and thought what would I do if I was called in to help with this? Moments later the phone rang and I was summonsed to an urgent meeting at New Scotland Yard.' Some of his colleagues were sent directly to the scene of the siege to escort and fetch whatever was required by the incident commander.

Directed to a location in inner London, the officer soon found himself at the entrance of a high-security building. When he entered, he quickly became engulfed in a special forces counter-terrorist rehearsal, which was not what he was expecting, and not something he'd been trained for. Meanwhile, two other officers were sent to his home to inform his wife that he wouldn't be back for several days. She was told not to worry; he was in safe hands.

'When I arrived at the location, I was greeted by a very confident and plucky young captain from the British Army,' he explained. 'I followed him into the building and through to a large yard. There standing before me was a full size building, built from timber, designed to replicate the Iranian Embassy.' A group of highly talented carpenters worked tirelessly to ensure that every detail of the embassy was exact. 'Soldiers climbed over the construction, swinging from ropes and jumping between rooms. I couldn't believe what I saw.' The officer was witnessing the SAS conduct a dress rehearsal of the attack that was to later conclude the siege. 'I was then taken into a briefing room. It was brimming with soldiers, maps, and impressive looking equipment. The captain gave me my instructions. I will take those to my grave.'

The SEG officer had been synchronized into the military heartbeat. Trusted, yes, essential, yes, expected, no, ready, yes. A close-knit, elite and secretive unit, the SAS don't bring guests into their camp unless absolutely required. It's not that they're not a friendly bunch, just that they wish to protect their methods and identities for the benefit of the public interest.

Their success is often determined by an element of surprise, combined with an unconventional inventiveness in the delivery of their operations. At the time of the siege, very few people knew that the SAS even existed. Their primary role of operating behind enemy lines required a level of individual professionalism and security of method that was best protected by being kept out of the public eye. The officer in question spent days with the soldiers, tirelessly rehearsing his part in an operation that thankfully never happened. In this kind of work plan Bs, Cs and so on are essential.

Back at the scene of the siege, police, military intelligence and surveillance teams had successfully identified those inside the building. The authorities now knew who the terrorists were, and who were hostages – an important if basic piece of information. Photos of those inside were issued to the SAS assault team. Faces were memorized. Drilling holes through the adjacent walls of the embassy allowed the surveillance teams to listen to conversations between the terrorists and hostages. An intelligence picture had formed. To rehearse the final details, a miniature 3D model of the embassy, and the positions of its occupants, was used to walk through the concluding elements of the assault. The SAS were now ready to take action. Once the operation was underway, every second would count. Life and death decisions would be made in an instant.

Negotiations continued until the body of a hostage was thrown from the main door of the embassy and onto the threshold. The terrorists threatened to kill a hostage every thirty minutes until their demands were met. At that point, Home Secretary William Whitelaw ordered that power be handed from the police to the military. Within minutes the SAS were launched into action and abseiled from the roof of the embassy before entering the building through the windows. Dressed from head to toe in black, and with their faces covered by gas masks, their arrival was followed by explosion, gunfire, and smoke bellowing from the windows. They had achieved the element of surprise. The assault, which was over within minutes, was heralded as a success, although tragically one hostage was killed by terrorist gunfire. Five of the six terrorists were shot dead inside the building by the SAS and the sixth was detained outside. The remaining hostages were moved to safety.

The operation, codenamed 'Nimrod', set a benchmark for counter-terrorist operations worldwide. The Metropolitan Police and the British Army had worked hand in hand and together they'd averted a disastrous outcome. Shy of media attention, the SAS had publicly exemplified their motto 'Who Dares Wins'. And the SEG had, once again, quietly demonstrated its utility at the sharp end of the British security community.

## The Pope's Visit

It's difficult to judge who would have been more shocked: the Pope, or the two drunks with whom he unwittingly came face-to-face. Whatever the case, the meeting probably shouldn't have happened.

Sitting having lunch in the canteen at New Scotland Yard, an urgent message crackled through the radio: 'immediate escort required for the Pope's convoy'. The Pope had been taken ill whilst attending a reception close to Victoria Station. 'We were told the Pope had left the reception and was now heading back to his residence,' recalled one of the SEG officers who had reacted to the radio message. 'Leaping on our bikes we did what we could to catch up with his convoy. Eventually we joined the vehicles in what was a less than desirable part of Battersea.' The vehicles were parked up at the side of the road outside a notoriously rough pub.

'We quickly discovered that the Pope's car had broken down,' continued the officer. 'As we got off our bikes we could see one of the protection officers transferring His Holiness to another vehicle. As the Pope stepped onto the kerb, two drunken Irishman staggered out of the pub to see what all the fuss was about, and clearly couldn't believe their eyes. Words were exchanged!'

The protection officer in question had determined that the two heavily-lubricated individuals were less of a problem if they weren't antagonized. The vino collapso had rendered them impolite and incomprehensible but not obviously violent. Pushing them away, either verbally or physically, may have escalated the situation, so the protection officer made a snap decision to handle them with humour. Despite a few unorthodox gestures from one of the drunks, they barely interrupted the Pope's transfer to the replacement vehicle.

The pastoral visit to the UK by His Holiness, Pope John Paul II in May 1982, was the first for a reigning pope in 400 years. The visit, which was the most important event for British Catholics since the Reformation, had almost been cancelled due to Britain's war with Argentina over the Falkland Islands. In a bid to not further antagonize the Roman Catholic majority in Argentina, an agreement was established that the visit would only go ahead on the understanding that the Pope would not meet with Prime Minister Margaret Thatcher.

During his six-day stay, the Pope travelled to England, Scotland and Wales. On landing at Gatwick Airport the first thing he did was kneel down to kiss the British tarmac. He then addressed the crowds and said: 'So I begin my pastoral visit to Britain with the words of Our Lord Jesus Christ. "Peace be with you. May the God of peace and reconciliation be with you all. May He bless your families and homes with His deep and abiding peace."' Visiting a total of nine cities, His Holiness delivered sixteen major addresses, to audiences of more than two million people. Although a national event, the security of the Pope's visit had been given to the Metropolitan Police to oversee the design of, and ultimately lead. In today's currency, the total cost of the visit was a little over twenty million pounds.

With the SEG covering all of the Pope's journeys in London, his first port of call was Westminster Cathedral. From there he travelled to meet HMQ at Buckingham Palace. He then held the first open-air mass at Wembley Stadium, which was attended by approximately 80,000 people. He was greeted by 350,000 people on arrival in Coventry. Travelling by helicopter to Liverpool, over one million people lined the route of his convoy all the way to the doors of the city's cathedral. Following a short stay in Scotland, where he attended seven venues and gave Holy Mass in Bellahouston Park his visit to the UK ended with a trip to Cardiff. On landing in Wales, he knelt to kiss the ground.

Security was at its highest, amplified due to an assassination attempt on His Holiness the previous year, on 13 May 1981. While addressing the public in St Peter's Square in the Vatican City, the Pope was hit by four bullets and suffered severe blood loss. He survived without serious injury but cancelled all overseas travel for nearly a year before visiting Portugal, followed immediately by the UK.

Planning for a visit of this magnitude begins months and, in some aspects, years ahead of time. Thousands of people from all over the country were involved and many hundreds of those were police. Several months prior to the Pope's arrival, a small number of Special Branch officers, along with PC Steve Brownridge from the SEG, were appointed to examine the various locations His Holiness planned to visit. 'I was summoned from the SEG office in Barnes to attend a meeting at New Scotland Yard,' recalled PC Brownridge. 'They said it was for an important assignment. On arrival, I was told that from this moment on, myself and a colleague from Traffic, were to visit all the locations in the Pope's schedule and conduct a security survey.' It wasn't long before PC Brownridge and his colleague were also asked to oversee the construction of the Popemobiles.

The vehicles, designed by a British firm called Ogle, based in Letchworth were built using a Range Rover and Leyland truck. Two were produced. PC Brownridge and his colleague developed the vehicles' exact security specifications following their recces. Having seen the locations, Brownridge surmised that the two vehicles would need to be easily armoured, made with bullet-proof glass, elegant with a dignified design and style befitting a man of his stature, powerful, quick, and capable of driving across rough ground.

The Pope himself would need to be visible, but safe. After writing up their requirements in a report, they presented their needs to the design company, who then produced the final vehicles. 'The project was relatively simple,' explained Tom Karen, then Managing Director of Ogle. 'We were briefed about the Pope's size and what steps suited him. The budget was adequate though time frame tight.' The problem was striking a balance between the police, who would have liked him to sit inside an armoured vehicle, and the church representatives who were keen for the Pope to be seen waving his arms to the crowd. 'The compromise was armoured glass leaving no more than his head and shoulders exposed,' added Karen. The vehicles, designed by Martin Smith (later to become Executive Director of Design at Ford Europe) were the first of their kind, setting a security standard and an iconic design, which are still used to this day.

Having completed the first tasks successfully, PC Brownridge and his colleague were then given the responsibility of becoming the Pope's lead protection drivers. The rest of the driving team comprised a mix of officers from the SEG and Special Branch.

The Pope's movements were a feat to control and coordinate. With a busy itinerary and scores of people desperate to see him, communication and careful planning were key. However, few of the senior public officials and religious figures with whom the Pope met during his visit had ever been responsible for hosting such a high-profile event. Even fewer of these individuals had any experience of working closely with the police. With all involved keen to capture as much of his time as possible, and multiple commitments locked into the diary, a strict schedule had to be maintained.

To the credit of all those responsible, the execution of the Pope's schedule unfolded with very few crinkles or creases. That said, there was perhaps one small ruffle! As one retired officer who was involved in the escorts explained:

'We had dropped the Pope and his SB [Special Branch] officer at an address in Westminster. According to the schedule, His Holiness was to stay at this address for three hours. In order to wait out the period and take a short dinner break, we went to the canteen at Canon Row Police Station. Just as we finished dinner and poured out the coffee, an emergency "ONTG" radio message arrived. [ONTG stands for 'Oh No They've Gone' and thankfully such messages are rare].

'We threw on our motorcycle gear and launched off to catch up with the convoy. We knew the route they would take, and estimated that we'd join them close to Chelsea Bridge. Moments before crossing the bridge we caught up with the convoy, and quickly slotted into position. To our horror, it was 'Chelsea cruise night', a monthly meeting of jacked-up cars and trucks, which happened by word of mouth, and attracted hundreds of spectators standing on the bridge. Luckily the Pope was travelling in a relatively low-key limousine, so it's unlikely anyone realized it was him.'

The slow-moving vehicles, and huge crowds of onlookers, presented many potential hazards to the convoy so the pace was increased. 'They were all treated to the sight of a complete protection team racing across the bridge,' laughed the officer.

## The Disarming and Disbanding Debacle

In August 1983, a badly thought out kneejerk reaction resulted in the SEG, and many other departments, being ordered to conduct all their operations without firearms. As a consequence, the group's bread-and-butter runs – prisoner court hearings and transfers – were handed over to specialist firearms teams. The decision was a police error of the gravest kind, and it was made due to events that happened at the beginning of the year.

On 14 January 1983, Metropolitan Police officers shot and seriously injured 26-year-old Stephen Waldorf, when he was misidentified as a dangerous and wanted criminal called David Martin. Martin was on the run having escaped a court cell in December 1982. He was wanted for a number of crimes, including shooting and seriously injuring a police officer in the summer of the previous year, while attempting to rob a cinema.

On 28 January, following a tip off from an informer, thirty-five officers were sent to Hampstead in London to arrest Martin. Having positively identified him in a busy Hampstead street, detectives spilled out from their vehicles to surround him. Spotting the officers, Martin, who was nicknamed 'Houdini' due to his ability to escape the authorities, ran into Hampstead Underground Station, jumped on a tube train and ran through the carriages. Officers were not far behind and arrested him in the tunnel between Hampstead and Belsize Park. Realizing Houdini would need extra precautions to ensure his secure custody, the SEG was called in to escort him to and from court and then to prison, where Martin was to serve just one year of his twenty-five year prison sentence before committing suicide in his cell. Stephen Waldorf would go on to make a full recovery and receive £150,000 compensation from the Metropolitan Police.

The mistake led to an internal review of how all armed police departments had been trained, asking the question whether or not they absolutely needed to carry firearms. The review was to take an uncomfortably long period of time, and until it was completed only the specialist firearm team known as D11 was to carry weapons. The decision to revoke permission for the SEG to carry guns led to high-level talks about dissolving the group as a specialist entity, sending officers back to their former postings and handing escort duties over to regular traffic units. For the first time in the SEG's history, the tone of talks caused morale to wane. The group's specialist and independent status was now under attack. As one retired officer said: 'For a moment it seemed that all the training and specialization we'd invested in was going to be thrown away. A number of my colleagues started to look for alternative positions within the police. I could hardly blame them.'

To help keep the group busy between VIP runs, the SEG was used for policing the new red routes and clearways during rush hours. During this period, the group received its first and only fixed penalty ticket since becoming permanent. It also undertook conventional convoy duties on motorcycles, escorting heavy and unusual loads through central London, usually from police border to police border. This work had been taken away from traffic garages and, as one officer clarified, transferring it to the SEG had gone down like a lead balloon: 'This was one of the only sources of their overtime. It was nearly all late turn work as the convoys could not start moving until after 8.00 pm.'

In January 1984 morale in the group was at an all-time low. Many officers were concerned that the group's ability to deliver high-security escorts had been massively compromised, and with no decision to re-arm on the horizon, the future of the SEG was looking increasingly doomed. But then, entirely unexpectedly, at the start of February a meeting between senior police officers concluded that the SEG would not be disbanded, or moved, and that additional duties, including the transfer of bullion, would soon be handed over the group.

Miraculously, the group's work picked up again and it became involved in escorting police officers to the north of England to support their Yorkshire Constabulary colleagues. The miners' strike in 1984 would also see the SEG increasingly in demand, as one former officer recalled:

'Every Sunday we supplied car escorts to thousands of officers being supplied to forces in the north of England to "assist" in manning the many picket lines at coal mines. I was on the first escorts and escorted about twenty coachloads of officers to a colliery in Yorkshire. On that first day you couldn't help be impressed by the sheer number of coaches and escorts and the number of separate convoys leaving Hendon for points north on the A1 and M1. These escorts became a regular duty every Sunday: lunch at Hendon and then off to the north. Usually took about twelve hours as a round trip as the coaches were very slow.'

By the start of 1985, permission to carry firearms was once again granted to the SEG. Business was back to normal.

## Murder of Yvonne Fletcher

'The siege is over. All the Libyans have left the embassy,' declared an official spokesperson for the Metropolitan Police following the eleven-day ordeal. The siege had begun following a tragic incident when, on 17 April 1984, Yvonne Fletcher, a 25-year-old police constable, was shot in the back whilst assisting at a protest outset the Libyan Embassy. Two gunmen were believed to have taken fire from within the confines of the embassy itself. A total of eleven Libyan protestors were also injured from the hail of bullets. Yvonne, who was taken by ambulance to a nearby hospital, died in surgery.

Yvonne Fletcher was among a number of police officers sent to the embassy to deal with a protest. This should have been routine business although no one had predicted, expected or planned for the level of violence that ensued. In his book *The Defence of the Realm*, Christopher Andrew wrote:

'Later in the day, following the shooting, the British Security Service learned that the Libyan embassy had proposed three options to its masters in Tripoli for dealing with the protestors;

i.    to clash directly with the demonstrations from outside the Bureau
ii.   to fire on them from inside the Bureau
iii.  to prevent the demonstration by diplomatic pressure'

The shooting of Yvonne Fletcher resulted in Britain ending all diplomatic relations with Libya. It was clear from the outset that the country's leader, Muammar Gaddafi, wasn't going to accept responsibility or cooperate with the British authorities. He and his team of embassy officials in London denied any knowledge of the shooting. British police and security forces surrounded the embassy and Gaddafi responded by directing his military to surround the British Embassy in Tripoli. A stalemate situation was upon them both, so seemingly the only option was to back down. The Home Secretary, having discounted the option of making arrests, struck an agreement to allow the embassy staff to return to Libya.

Once again, the SEG found itself in the heart of history in the making. It was given responsibility leading the large team of specialist police departments, which had been formed to support the escort of thirty embassy staff to the airport. The strong possibility of the convoy being attacked by anti-Gaddafi groups meant that the highest level of security was called for. PC Trevor Pryke was part of the escort. 'The convoy included a police bus from the Special Patrol Group and a second bus and car from Diplomatic Patrol Group,' he recalled. 'The police helicopter was also overhead for most of the run.'

When you drive in convoy with another vehicle it can be difficult to stay together, and the longer the convoy, the greater the challenge. Although the journey between the Libyan Embassy and Heathrow Airport was expected to take a little under thirty minutes, the route would follow busy main roads and a motorway, crossing scores of traffic lights, roundabouts and junctions. There were plenty of places for an attack to be mounted.

Convoy drivers have to compensate for each other at every stop, obstacle, junction and turn. The lead driver cannot think in singular but, rather, as if they're towing along carriages. If they don't adapt their driving style, they risk breaking the convoy apart and leaving a vehicle sitting at a red traffic light or a busy junction, whilst they steam ahead. Drive too close and your vision ahead will be impaired and you raise the risk of knocking into the rear of the vehicle ahead if it has to brake suddenly. Leave too large a gap between cars, and a public vehicle, or possibly an attacker, could slip between the convoy, breaking the flow and distance and increasing further the risk of separation.

The route had the convoy travelling along the A4 towards Heathrow, joining the M4 at Chiswick. Just short of Heathrow, the convoy stopped at the Civil Service College and government officials interviewed the passengers. They waited at the college until receiving word that the aircraft was ready.

As there had been little time to make decisions during the siege, hardly any planning could take place. The convoy included an unusually large number of vehicles and this would require high levels of coordination. But coordination wasn't the only thing troubling the group. One or possibly two of the embassy staff within the convoy were more than likely to be responsible for the murder of Yvonne Fletcher. She was a fellow police officer and one of their own. It was only natural for officers to feel conflicted. Although they wanted to do a good job, they also wondered why we were letting the suspects go. Was this our only option? The officers knew that once the convoy reached the airport, their passengers – and probable murderers – would be beyond the long arm of the law. As they sat on their bikes at the edge of the airfield waiting for the plane to take off, you wouldn't have blamed them for wishing for some sort of technical failure so the aircraft would remain on the ground, giving the government more time to seek out an alternative course. However, the wheels went up and the plane rose without a hitch.

Intelligence hadn't been shared efficiently, and the British government had played its hand badly. Despite an unrelenting police investigation, to this day no individual has been brought to justice for the murder of Yvonne Fletcher.

**The Harrods Bomb**

In the midst of the Christmas shopping period, the bomb blast outside London's luxury department store Harrods on 17 December 1983 achieved its intent. Killing three civilians, and three police officers, it also injured ninety people. A police dog handler lost both legs and a part of his hand in the explosion. His search dog was killed. The IRA claimed responsibility for the wicked crime. Just seven days before, the IRA detonated a bomb at the Royal Artillery Barracks injuring three soldiers. London was on high alert.

The thirty-pound bomb was planted in a 1972 blue Austin 1300 GT, parked near the side of the entrance of Harrods on Hans Crescent. Hundreds of shoppers would pass through the entrance every hour. Just thirty-seven minutes prior to the explosion, the IRA called the London branch of the Samaritans charity, using a recognized code word, which helped confirm the call wasn't a hoax. Police arriving on the scene were presented with scores of vehicles to check. A registration number was given, but not a description of the car. As the first responders began to conduct their search the bomb detonated.

Moments following the explosion, the IRA made a second telephone call claiming that another bomb had been left in the C&A fashion store on Oxford Street. The area was cordoned off and searched, but the threat turned out to be a hoax. Following the incidents, a decision was made to double the number of police officers in high-intensity areas, and increase the availability of bomb squads across central London. The physical security of locations believed to be vulnerable to attack was also upped significantly.

Immediately, work began on repairing the damage to Harrods' façade. Just three days later, defiant in the face of terrorism, the store re-opened. Hundreds of eager shoppers lined the street outside. A number of high-profile individuals, celebrities and public officials also attended the opening, including Elton John and Margaret Thatcher's husband Denis. The British public's resilience to terrorism has always been remarkable. Security at the opening was boosted significantly and Harrods welcomed the increased measures with open arms, allowing undercover police officers to patrol the interior of the building disguised as shoppers.

A large number of police were involved in the immediate aftermath of the bombing. One of those officers recalled how, on the day of the attack, he'd helped control traffic and set up security cordons around the store, while his colleagues helped gather crucial evidence.

'After a long day at Harrods I managed to get to a dinner with the SEG, which had been arranged months before. I had been part time with the group and was planning to apply to become a full-time member. As I arrived at the location, a boat moored in St Katharine Docks, the group were already awaiting my arrival and as I walked on to the deck they all stood to attention and raised a glass in memory of the people who had died earlier that day. Grown men do cry.'

Two years later, in September 1985, a police memorial was unveiled on Harrods' wall in memory of the officers killed. Now a fully-fledged member of the SEG, the same officer would take part in the unveiling. 'I knew from an earlier briefing that my team and I would be escorting Princess Alexandra to the unveiling ceremony,' he recalled. 'It was to be a high-security event.' Following the run, the SEG team was invited to join Princess Alexandra for tea at St James's Palace, where she took the opportunity to thank them for their work and to share some thoughts about the day. 'A thank you from such a lovely lady was priceless.'

## Escorting the Monarch (Again)

The British Monarchy had, for centuries, enjoyed a great deal of freedom whilst moving around the country. Although ceremonial events commanded all the trimmings of horse-drawn carriages, honour guards and cavalry escorts, everyday journeys were far more low key.

By the early 1980s, many members of the royal family had started to employ the services of the SEG on a regular basis. Although HMQ had experienced the benefit of an SEG escort from time to time, only three vehicles were allowed – no easy-rider – and she had opted against using them on a routine basis. On such occasions foot patrol officers were still used to control traffic and traffic lights, at busy junctions. The following is an annotation from a letter sent to group by a member of the Queen's staff:

> '15th February 1980 – 'The Queen has asked me to thank the three officers that facilitated Her Majesty's journey from London to Windsor this evening. I should be glad if you would pass the message on and add my praise for the skill with which the operation was carried out. I took the opportunity throughout the journey to point out the unobtrusiveness of the escort and I think the point was taken. Certainly the Queen was grateful; it is perhaps a little early to say she is converted, but she was impressed.'

The Queen, and her husband, HRH Prince Philip, the Duke of Edinburgh 'preferred to keep to the old methods,' explained a retired inspector in charge of SEG. 'If HMQ was to travel between Buckingham Palace and Paddington Railway Station by car, all the traffic junctions between those two locations would need to be manned by as many as fifty police officers in advance of the journey.' The officers would wait patiently at the junction, keeping a look out for a royal limousine bearing an illuminated light on the roof. The light would identify the car as HMQ's. The officer would then start controlling and stopping the traffic so the royal car could pass by unhindered. The system was expensive and inefficient and not without the risk of mistakes. For example, on foggy or rainy days it could be difficult, even impossible, to identify the royal vehicle in time to control traffic.

It is often discussed in police protection circles that HMQ was concerned that the SEG's methods disrupted the public too much for her liking. One officer explained how 'she had an image of us forcing cars off the road to allow the convoy to pass through. We worked hard to show her that wasn't the case.' Others are of the view that her personal staff wished to see and hear the experiences of other royals before suggesting that HMQ employ the group. Whatever the reason, by the start of 1984 her mind had changed, and the SEG was given responsibility for escorting her on all routine journeys. We may not ever know if there was any single event that caused this change. However, we do know that there are several factors that contributed to it.

Any concerns that the SEG's methods were some way unsuitable were debunked when HMQ and Prince Phillip were escorted from Heathrow Airport to Buckingham Palace during a London-wide power cut. With the majority of traffic lights out, a decision was made to include four of the most experienced SEG motorcyclists to escort the royals. The addition of the fourth bike meant that an easy rider could be placed at the head of the royal car, allowing the remaining three bikes to engage the highly effective leapfrogging technique.

One can only imagine how much cleaning, polish and checking over of motorcycles and uniforms was done that day. The four escorts arrived at Buckingham Palace an hour or so before departing to collect the Monarch, to run over details and help prepare her driver. Foot duty officers at junctions were stood down, so the system of leapfrogging would have to be employed throughout the run. This was to be first time HMQ would experience such an escort and all involved were apprehensive of her reaction. The royal driver would need to alter his driving style accordingly. Following a lecture in the quadrangle of the palace, they embarked on their outward journey, using the opportunity to practise further en route to Paddington. When they were as ready as they could be, they waited patiently for their passengers at the royal collection point at the station. Nervous – maybe; excited – possibly; proud – definitely.

With minimal disruption to traffic, and a great deal of elegance, the royal car reached the palace in record time. 'Shortly after this escort we received word from the palace that HMQ was extremely happy with us, and we were to expect more runs with her in the future,' explained a retired officer who had ridden one of the four motorcycles on that historic day. Around the same time, legend has it that a well-respected and famously grumpy Scottish police officer wrote a letter of complaint to the palace. The officer in question was responsible for managing all foot patrol officers in the area around Buckingham Palace. His letter is said to have highlighted the heavy financial implications of employing foot officers to man junctions in advance of HMQ's journey. Furthermore, he is said to have outlined the costs, numbers of officers and time spent to support a journey from Buckingham Palace to Paddington Station. The letter, which is said to have reached HMQ herself, concluded with a simple question – why not use the SEG?

With many of her own family already employing, and greatly valuing, the services of the group, it was no surprise that word of its potential disbandment reached her. She would have understood that her endorsement of the SEG would end any discussions of disbanding them. Maybe it was just coincidence but from hereon she used the group on a regular basis. The impact was great. 'Suddenly we found ourselves overwhelmed with requests for escorts,' explained a retired officer. The relationship between the SEG and the dignitaries it accompanied was also changing. 'Many of them were intrigued to meet us in person, to speak with us, and find out more about the team who escorted the Monarch,' he added.

With the final, and by far most prestigious, jewel now placed securely in the crown, the group had not only achieved the highest level of royal approval, but had also secured its future.

## The Brighton Bombing

'You have to be lucky all the time. We only have to be lucky once.'
IRA statement following the Brighton Bomb at the Conservative Party Conference.

Rarely in its history has the group been required to provide escorts to members of parliament. Occasionally, however, on high-profile occasions, or where a specific threat has been identified, assistance has been called upon. Such an occasion followed the IRA bombing of the Conservative Party Conference at the Grand Hotel in Brighton on 12 October 1984.

The security services had warned Whitehall for several years that the IRA wanted to attack a Conservative Party conference. On this occasion, Patrick Magee, a wanted IRA bomber, succeeded. Evading police security searches, a long-delay bomb, planted inside the hotel nearly three weeks earlier, detonated just metres away from the bedrooms of the majority of the government's cabinet ministers. Ripping through the upper floors of the hotel, the bomb blast left a huge, gaping hole in the heart of the building. The primary target, Margaret Thatcher, survived the attack, materializing from the crumbling building entirely unscathed. Tragically, five members of her party were killed in the blast and a further thirty-one injured, some seriously.

Despite the expectations of many, Thatcher ordered the conference to continue. Standing before her party, many of whom were still shaken and traumatized by the events of the previous night, she said: 'The fact that we are gathered here now, shocked but composed and determined, is a sign not only that this attack has failed, but that all attempts to destroy democracy by terrorism will fail.' Here was a prime minister who had sent troops to war against Argentina to reclaim the Falkland Islands against the advice of her own staff, and won. Her economic policy was pulling, tearing and weaving new patterns into the fabric of society. Beloved by many and despised by lots, she was an exceptionally divisive politician. For those who supported her, she'd achieved a status close to royalty – many claiming that the UK now had two monarchs. Despite the threats, she was now standing firmly and defiantly against her would-be murderers, the IRA.

Following the conference, the SEG was called by Special Branch to quietly collect and escort Thatcher to her country residence, Chequers. An officer involved recalled the events of the day: 'We'd been told that Margaret Thatcher wasn't keen on an escort. The reason given was that she was worried about the safety of the motorcyclists, and therefore couldn't concentrate on her official papers on the journey home.' It's hard to believe after everything she'd been through, this would have been a concern but it gave an insight into her kindness. In daytime traffic, the journey would usually take a little over two hours, but by employing a mixture of high-security convoy tactics using both cars and motorcycles, it took the group just under an hour and twenty minutes. On arrival at Chequers, she invited the officers in for tea and took time to thank them for bringing her home 'so swiftly and so safely'.

## The Gold Rush

The transfer of valuable assets between the Bank of England (BoE) and secure storage locations around the UK had, for many years, been the responsibility of a dedicated team of security officers at the bank's HQ in the City of London. Their work had been exemplary, but as the security environment became more demanding, decisions were made to hand it over to the Metropolitan Police. The job was given to the SEG.

A fifth of the world's gold is under guard in London. The gold sitting in the BoE vaults is said to be worth approximately £180 billion. The keys used to access the vaults are three foot long and are thought to be far more secure than any electronic options currently on the market. Little has changed since the day in the mid 1980s when one of the group's team leaders (a sergeant) was sent to negotiate the handover with the existing security staff.

The techniques used to transfer the bank's assets are a closely-guarded secret, and the BoE's own security team was reluctant to hand them over without assurance that they would be adhered to properly. 'I needed a diplomat,' explained the inspector in charge of SEG at the time. 'My other sergeants were good but I needed someone who could be persuasive without upsetting what was a sensitive and complicated situation. It was a tough ask, but I knew the man for the job, I knew he could do it.' His instinct proved right, and despite initially meeting with a frosty reception, the sergeant was quick to win them over. With the handover a success, BoE runs were soon underway.

The BoE responsibility brought a great deal of work to the group, allowing it to recruit several additional staff. The runs were also well received by the group and made for a change from the routine. 'Some of my favourite runs were with the BoE,' explained a former officer. 'We never actually knew exactly what we were escorting, but whatever was in the vans, it was probably worth more than my entire life's pay.' Although a great deal of effort was made to ensure the runs were low key, any would-be criminal worth their salt would recognize that the convoy was a potentially valuable target. Due to the high monetary value of the loads, every possible layer of security was incorporated into the runs, often working in partnership with other specialist teams from across the police.

## A New Communication System

Throughout the mid to late 1980s, the group began to experiment with a new range of crash helmets and mobile radio communication systems. Whilst on the move, communication between the escorts was achieved visually in silence, with a combination of hand signals, road positioning, motorcycle posture, observation of brake lights, and a general experience of routines. Almost like reading body language and lip reading, communication was subtle but, with practice, became instinctive and highly effective. 'Officers placed in cars could communicate via radio whilst on the move but the motorcyclists didn't,' explained a retired team leader. 'Before in-helmet communications, the radios fitted to our motorcycles were only used to contact base.'

The first mobile communication systems were installed into open-face helmets. The microphone extended out of the helmet on a short boom. For obvious reasons, they were less than ideal, as one officer explained: 'They picked up lots of wind noise, making it difficult to hear at times. If it rained the boom got wet and would trouble the microphone.' Both open flip lid and full-faced closed helmets were tried out. The full-faced helmet won hands down and was introduced to the group. The introduction of in-helmet radio communication meant that in certain scenarios the team could work quicker and more efficiently. Mindful of the risks of an adversary listening in, communication was kept to a minimum and over time, a coded language was adopted. Radio talk was reserved largely to the occasional joke or cleverly-placed jibe. The system of silence developed over three decades kept observational skills sharp. If it ain't broke, don't fix it.

PC Gerry Mobbs, storeman and regular group escort recalled how 'despite its benefits, the new helmet had one major downside – we couldn't use the whistle satisfactorily as it was now inside the helmet.' This was the most essential part of the group's kit so the problem had to be fixed quickly. Fortunately, PC Mobbs had a brainwave. 'I had some left over plastic medi-tubes from the first aid kits so I started experimenting with them, bending and cutting them into shape until they were the right length. With the whistle mouthpiece forced onto one end, it now sat outside the helmet, just below the chin.' The solution worked perfectly and is still used today.

**Taking a Punt**

In 1988, King Juan Carlos of Spain, accompanied by his wife Queen Sophia, was invited to receive an honorary doctorate at Cambridge University. He was in good company as former recipients included Albert Einstein, General Eisenhower, Field Marshal Montgomery, Mother Teresa and Nelson Mandela. For a number of the escorts this was another opportunity to work with the royal couple, having been part of the Spanish state visit team two years earlier. The programme in 1986 had been a landmark in improved relations between the two countries, who had been arguing over Gibraltar, and it was the first state visit by the Spanish Monarchy for eighty-one years.

Arriving in London and following a series of official welcomes, the entourage left for Cambridge in a convoy led by the SEG. The route beyond London was relatively straightforward and the officers were familiar with the journey. As one explained:

'When a head of state came to the UK on official business they'd often want to visit a son or daughter studying at one of the ancient universities. Sometimes it was a chance for the VIP to visit their own college or look towards placing a child in later years. Trips to Oxford or Cambridge were popular and we would be required to take them.'

Although there were no known threats to the royal couple whilst in the UK, an escort provided an extra level of assurance that their visit would take place uneventfully.

After delivering the royal couple to the university with their close protection officers, the escorts found themselves with a couple of hours free. Parking their vehicles at a secure designated location, they changed out of uniform and some decided to explore the city while their sergeant stayed with the vehicles. 'We wandered into town and someone suggested that we sit by the river and watch the punt boats pass by,' explained one of the officers. They found a bench and sat among the tourists and students eating their lunchtime sandwiches.

'Everything went well until we heard "Oh no!"' continued the officer. 'We looked on to discover that a romantic couple had lost their punt pole, which was now sticking out of the river about ten foot away from their boat.' Luckily an emergency paddle was supplied so, with some difficulty and through tears of laughter, the young captain – who was dressed in a straw boater – regained direction and recovered the pole. 'By now we'd finished our lunch so we decided to walk back to the vehicles,' added the officer. 'Looking back for one last look, we could see they were off again, paddle firmly at the ready, but heading off with little control.' The officers stood on the famous Magdalene Bridge and watched the couple float towards them. 'As they passed underneath we had to shout to Straw Hat to duck as he was about to be swept off.'

Having rejoined their colleagues and vehicles, they noticed that in the rear of the Range Rover, next to neat uniforms and highly-polished boots, was a cardboard box peppered with tiny holes. A slight scuffling came from within. One of the heroes bravely decided to have a peek only to discover a bantam chick looking up and chirping away. The sergeant, a poultry enthusiast, had found the bird limping along the path into town with a slightly damaged wing. Now there was one small extra passenger for the return trip.

On the journey to London, using newly-acquired in-helmet communications, the officers exchanged jokes about events, the straw hat and the fluffy new recruit. Later, at Heathrow Airport, the escorts were presented to the King and Queen of Spain. Hands were shaken and cufflinks bearing the symbol of the Spanish Monarchy were presented as gifts to each officer. It was a wonderful ending to a most interesting visit. And the bantam? Named 'Carlos', this university-bred bird grew to maturity, fathered several lively daughters and lived to a good age in suburban London.

## The SEG Christmas

As is common in police circles, the end of year is celebrated with a family-friendly Christmas party. The SEG is no different. Attending as a child, I remember a great deal of effort was put into the occasion. As well as a large and brightly decorated Christmas tree, there were colourful lights, paper chains, wreaths – the lot. I remember sitting on Santa's lap and receiving a tiny toy motorcycle which I kept by my bedside for years. Many of the guests knew each other well, so the atmosphere was warm and welcoming. We all felt like one of the SEG family. The evening would often start out with a tour of the garage, with finger food and festive music playing in the background, followed by Santa's circle, which is when the children would line up to receive a small gift. The kids would then be invited to roam freely around the garage. Most of us would congregate inside the games room – a large room containing two full-size snooker tables and a dartboard. However, I liked to listen in on the stories.

With a drink in their hands, officers would regale colleagues with stories of unusual escorts, fun moments and outstanding achievements. They gave an incredible insight into the work of the group and its enviable team spirit. The Christmas party was also a time for recognition, and honours were handed out by team leaders. The Marco Polo award, named after the thirteenth-century explorer, was bestowed as and when required – which was normally every couple of years – to 'whoever mistakenly took a convoy off course'. Nearly every member of the group would receive it at some point. Most of the officers were involved in up to three escorts a day, and with two or three teams out on the road each day, the occasional mistake did happen.

Not all the awards were jokey: one was given for the hardest worker. Usually escorts of dignitaries require at least three motorcycles, sometimes more, depending on traffic and various other factors. However, on one occasion, for reasons unknown, Australian Prime Minister Malcolm Fraser was to only receive two motorcycle escorts for his journey between central London and Heathrow Airport. With eight Daimlers in convoy, travelling much of the journey on the offside of the road, the two officers managed, miraculously, to escort him without delay directly to the VIP suite. As the officers stood on the red carpet at the foot of his plane with their bikes, the prime minister, surprised to see such skeletal accompaniment, came up to the two men and said: 'Bloody hell, where's the rest of yer? I thought there were hundreds yer.'

Stories would come thick and fast at these parties. One officer held up a photo of himself and colleagues stood next to a mounted glass frame in a London museum. On this occasion, the group had escorted the Shroud of Turin, a cloth commonly believed to have belonged to Jesus. The officer explained how the cloth had been moved between locations as discreetly as possible so as not to raise attention to its exact whereabouts. I was awestruck that some of the people beside me had encountered this priceless artefact in such an intimate way and yet the story was told with no boasting or drama.

My eyes and mouth were wide open as the officer went on to explain that during a visit to Britain in 1988, President Ronald Reagan had walked out of his residence at Winfield House in Regent's Park fifteen minutes earlier than expected. As he approached his limousine, a member of the SEG explained to his personal chief of security that the president wouldn't be able to depart until the agreed time. In response, the chief security officer said 'the President of the United States of America will leave when he wants to leave.' Reagan, who'd overheard the exchange, turned and walked back to the house. 'Even the President of the USA knew that arriving early to meet Her Majesty wasn't an option,' laughed the officer.

Not all stories related to recent events. A retired member stepped forward to regale us with some tales. 'Whilst en route to Windsor Castle from an appointment in the countryside, we reached a point in a winding lane which was completely impassable,' he said. 'Moments prior, farmers had driven tractors across the lane creating mountains of snow, which could only be cleared with a snowplough.' The group's passenger was no other than HMQ. 'Thinking quickly, I jumped out of the protection car and ran over to a pub nestled a few yards back from the edge of the lane.' The officer, who was on his first escort with the Queen, asked to speak with the landlord. 'An elderly gentlemen appeared from behind the bar and invited me to explain my predicament.' It was obvious the landlord didn't believe a word he'd said but a moment later the door opened and in walked the Queen herself. 'Astonished, the landlord shuffled up to her, gave a somewhat clumsy curtsey, and invited her to wait upstairs in his private quarters, where she was to sit by a small electric radiator, enjoy a cup of tea, and enjoy a bite of traditional pub food – a rare treat for a queen – for nearly an hour.'

The food at SEG events was always very good – especially the Christmas gingerbread cookies. One of the officer's daughters had been baking cookies for years. It all started when she'd made a batch for a school project. Leaving the house before sunrise, her dad pinched a handful and took them to the garage. After being spotted by colleagues, the cookies were slowly prised away from his clutches until every last one had gone. Popular and now in high demand, requests travelled back home and the daughter got to work. She continued to make the cookies for nearly two decades, with special batches for state visits. 'I was told the test of quality was if they survived being thrown between moving vehicles,' laughed an officer. The baker's father was responsible for carrying the mobile tuck shop. As escorts would leapfrog ahead he'd throw them a boiled sweet as they zoomed by – a difficult but entirely achievable trick learnt in training days with the MPT. On one occasion, while sitting lined up in Sussex Gardens waiting for HMQ to walk out of Paddington Station, his bag of boiled sweets spilt out of his jacket, scattering over the street – much to the amusement of bystanders and fellow escorts. His daughter said she wished her dad had kept to cookies: 'He was finally relieved of tuck shop duties when he fell off his bike in front of Princess Anne,' she revealed, 'and his pick n' mix spilled out all over the road.'

On rare occasions accidents would happen and some, sadly, have led to life-altering injuries. Officers who suffered such a fate are always remembered and their privacy is respected. Thankfully, most accidents have only led to minor injuries, if any at all. One such occasion, which was revisited during a Christmas party, concerned PC Peter Skerritt. 'I hadn't been full time in the group for all that long, and at the time I was sharing a motorcycle with my supervisor, the team leader,' he recalled. 'I think I was the first non-traffic officer on the group so some were sceptical about my suitability.' Having completed several months at the garage and proved his abilities, he was now allowed to participate in a royal escort. 'I took up the position of one of the leapfroggers and we were to escort Prince Charles to his residence at Kensington Palace.'

The journey started perfectly and when they were about half a mile away from Kensington Palace Gardens, PC Skerritt went to overtake the Bentley to get ahead of the convoy and find a route through the traffic. 'Shortly after passing the vehicle I was T-boned by a car doing an unexpected U-turn in the middle of the road.' Peter had no warning. The driver of the car had failed to use his indicators so he didn't even have a chance to brake. Fortunately, Peter was travelling at a relatively low speed. 'I somersaulted over the windshield of the bike, briefly onto the bonnet of the car, before doing another forward roll and onto the road,' he recalled. 'The continuing forward momentum then carried me to my feet. I turned around to find myself looking directly into the rear seat of the Bentley and to see Prince Charles, mouth open and eyes on stalks, having witnessed the whole crunch.' Peter's bike was badly damaged but as the escort passed him by he gave a thumbs up to show he wasn't seriously injured. 'After the royal car glided by I sank to the ground in a state of shock and sat myself on the kerbside. The convoy continued to the palace whereupon Charles rushed over to my colleagues asking if I was ok – and offered to send the Bentley back for me.' Evidently concerned, Charles wrote him the following letter:

*'Peter, I thought you might need a little "medicine" to repair any damage sustained when you came off your motorcycle the other day! I was so relieved to see you jump up straight away off the ground, but do hope any neck and back injuries will soon be healed. All best wishes, Charles '*

The bike Peter was riding on that day had the numberplate R123 SEG. He remembered it clearly because the supervisor with whom he shared the bike presented him with its blue lights (which was just about all that was remaining) as a memento. As the story concluded, another officer, who was standing at the back of the room enjoying the festivities, shouted out: 'Sometime in the distant past, one of the old boys is said to have fallen off his motorcycle some metres ahead of a convoy. Whilst sat on the ground licking his wounds, seeing the convoy approach, he sat bolt upright and saluted the royal car as it passed him by.'

I also had my own story to tell, which I shared with the other kids with a great deal of pride. One day, my dad told my mum that a convoy was to pass by my local school. His passenger was Princess Anne and it was her birthday. Recently divorced, she was celebrating by attending a series of official commitments. One of the group had placed a birthday card on her seat, which she opened and read cheerily whilst sitting in the vehicle. The convoy approached exactly on time – just as my dad said it would. As it grew closer I remember thinking how it looked like a flock of swans flying low across a lake. The first face I could make out was that of my dad's. He was sat at the front of the convoy on a gleaming white motorcycle. I stood by the side of the street together with my mum and my nan, and a large group of kids and teachers. We waved and shouted 'Happy birthday'. The princess turned, looking a little surprised at the intervention, and waved back with a beaming smile. Later she asked: 'Who were those people? Why did they know I was passing by? And how did they know it was my birthday?' Having been told the finer details of the unscheduled operation, she smiled and with a warm and happy look in her eyes, continued to her next engagement.

Just days before the Christmas party in 1988, the Lockerbie Pan Am flight bombing had shocked the world. A special incident room at Heathrow Airport Police Station had been set up to assist with the investigation. Bob Caswell, former SEG officer turned official driver for Police Commissioner Sir Peter Imbert planned to take him to meet with police staff at Heathrow to help boost morale. Just as they set off on their journey, they received notice that the incident room had been closed down at short notice, and that the entire operation was to move immediately to Scotland. At this news, Sir Peter said, 'What are we going to do now?' to which Bob responded by recommending they attend the SEG Christmas party in Barnes. Sir Peter agreed. Using the car phone, Bob rang ahead to the garage at Barnes to advise them that he would be bringing Sir Peter to the group party. 'The message was naturally taken with a pinch of salt,' explained PC Paul Mellor, the officer who'd taken the call and assumed it was a festive prank.

A little earlier, one of the sergeants had been changing from uniform into his evening suit only to discover that he'd left his jacket at home. PC

Mellor stepped in. 'Being a helpful sort of chap, I was able to provide my supervisor with a jacket in order to maintain his usual smart appearance,' he said. 'The jacket was bright red with white fur piping – the top half of my Father Christmas costume.' The sergeant, now downstairs in the basement greeting guests and organizing parking, was the first to see the commissioner's Jaguar with Bob Caswell sitting in the front seat. 'Bob was seen to put his head in his hands,' explained Paul. Realizing who was in the back seat, the sergeant stepped forward and opened the door for Sir Peter. As Sir Peter climbed out, Santa stood to attention and said – as is routine when a senior officer appears – 'All correct Sir,' to which Sir Peter replied 'Thank you Father Christmas' before being led away by Bob to enjoy the party. Since Bob's call had been taken as a wind up, no one was expecting Sir Peter to actually walk into the room. As he did, everything came to a standstill, and a deathly silence ensued, until PC Mellor's wife saved the day by stepping forward and saying: 'Welcome to the SEG Sir, and thank you for presenting my husband with his long service medal last month.'

Another story, which was told by the inspector in charge of the group, referred to an official visit of the Australian Prime Minister Bob Hawke in the late 1980s. Hawke and his wife Hazel were staying at the Hyde Park Hotel in Knightsbridge. Traditionally, at the end of any visit, the escorting team would line up and be introduced to the head of state. Usually this happens at the airport, but on this occasion it took place in the lobby of the hotel. With the bikes and officers lined up neatly at the entrance, the inspector in charge walked to the threshold and waited patiently for the prime minister and his wife to materialize. Catching sight of the couple approaching, the inspector turned to give notice to his officers. To his horror, they had stuck corks on strings to the peaks of their crash helmets. By now it was too late to do anything but the inspector needn't have worried. The prime minister and his wife took the joke in good spirit and found it all very amusing.

We families of the SEG officers understood how serious, and potentially hazardous, the roles of our loved ones could be We also recognized their exceptional reputation and privileged status within the Metropolitan Police. Just like the group, we didn't dwell on either of these factors. While these stories brought it home to everyone that the job carried immense danger, they were told with amusement and were enjoyed by all. The knack of making light of something serious was another example of the group's unique habit of facing adversity with humour.

Over the years, the group received hundreds of Christmas cards from all sorts of important people, including members of the royal family, politicians, senior military figures, as well as their partner police departments. One day, PC Peter Skerritt suggested to the management that it might be an idea to return the compliment. 'They agreed, and being a bit handy with Photoshop I took on the task.' Following much discussion, it was decided that the first card would have a Hollywood movie theme. 'So, I took an image of an SEG officer sitting on his bike and photoshopped Arnold Schwarzenegger's face into position,' recalled Peter. 'I sent the cards out to all the royals, the prime minister, cabinet ministers as well as various government departments we worked closely with.' In total 160 cards were sent out, all handwritten, and funded from the pockets of the group through its communal tea club. Needless to say, the cards were well received.

The following year more cards were produced. Despite receiving good wishes from many of the royals, the group had never received a card from HMQ and, concerned that it had upset protocol, decided to remove the Queen from the list. As a side note, Her Majesty receives approximately 60,000 pieces of correspondence every year and can't possibly read or respond to all. A week or two after the new cards went out, Peter received a phone call from HMQ's private secretary asking why she hadn't received one. 'He politely put my mind to rest so I quickly went about sending one of the cards to the palace,' explained Peter. 'She was immediately put back on the top of the list. She didn't send us a card in return but we did receive a letter, again from her private secretary, saying how much she enjoyed it.'

Every year the cards became increasingly elaborate and ever more popular. Eventually they were so well known that to receive one became a huge honour. One year the royal mews staff were keen to be involved in the production – they had an idea. Peter elaborated: 'After dropping off a member of the royal family, we were quickly ushered into a courtyard and asked to line up in pairs on our bikes in front of a royal carriage just outside the coach houses.' The carriage was originally built for Queen Victoria but had recently been used for Christmas charity events to deliver presents to sick children. 'With the help of a few personal hours at home working on Photoshop (including removing the wheels of the carriage and changing the coach house number to 007), the rest, as they say, is history.'

**BMW R80 (1980-1990 approx).** The first of a series of BMW motorcycles employed by the SEG. The R80, with its powerful and quick 800cc boxer twin engine, produced a useful 50bhp. Leg shields provided protection from the weather and the smooth engine reduced vibration, making the overall ride a more refined experience. Furthermore, unlike the Triumphs, it didn't leak oil. A radio and handset were attached to the fuel tank. The rear box cutting edge electrics offered bright lights (useful for signalling to oncoming traffic) and a reliable electric starter, relegating kick starting to the history books. During November of 1987 Prince William and Prince Harry spent an afternoon at the SEG garage in Barnes where they were both photographed sitting aloft a BMW R80. Perhaps this was also when the boys received their first motorcycle lesson!

# The 1990s

## A New Dawn

*You're sitting in your car en route to the garage. This afternoon marks the end of Margaret Thatcher's premiership as prime minister and today you're escorting her to Buckingham Palace so she can give notice of resignation to HMQ.*

*It's 8.30 am and it's going to be a nice day for November. Stuck in traffic you check your watch. The back route you normally take is closed due to unannounced maintenance of the road. You're annoyed because the delay will set you back several important minutes. There's a small competition running between colleagues in the garage over who can get to work the quickest and you've definitely lost today. Turning on the radio in search of traffic news you wonder how many other thousands of Londoners are stuck on their way to work. The city you live in is fast becoming one of the most cosmopolitan on the planet. It is also becoming one of the most congested. Ejecting the latest Phil Collins album from the CD player, you begin flicking through radio stations, but you struggle to find anything that doesn't burn your ears. This isn't going to be another day in paradise.*

*Trapped, there's nothing to do but sit and look at the mass of unfamiliar faces exiting Baker Street Underground Station. Red double decker buses and an articulated lorry block the view, but as you edge over to look ahead, all you can see are vehicles. With the arrival of cheap airlines and the opening of the Eurotunnel, tourism has increased substantially bringing more pedestrians and traffic to the streets of London. The tired, expensive railway and uncomfortable underground system have pushed more people on to the roads to negotiate the city's complex one-way system. As you sit pondering the day ahead you decide that tomorrow you'll take the motorcycle to work.*

*Arriving at the garage with just enough time to have a cup of tea, you change into uniform and begin preparing your motorcycle. Whilst giving the bike a final polish, you think about the moments leading up to Thatcher's resignation. Your colleagues are ready and you head off to Downing Street to collect the PM. On arrival, you are guided to a position immediately in front of Number 10 and stop to rest just ahead of the prime ministerial Jaguar. The black, shiny door opens and out comes Margaret Thatcher for the last time as prime minister. She has a tear in her eye. Her tenure had come to a somewhat brutal end. At times controversial, and with a contentious style, her legacy continues to divide public opinion. Thirteen years later her funeral cortege would also receive an escort, but this time for security purposes as well as ceremonial.*

Margaret Thatcher's resignation on 22 November, 1990 triggered more than a change in leadership – it led to the slow decay and eventual demise of the then Conservative Party. Her successor, John Major, was to remain as leader for seven years. By the end of his term, in 1997, the party had collapsed around him. The change to Labour, and the leadership of Tony Blair, would result in a shift in the security climate, especially in light on his decisions pertaining to Iraq. Blair would become the first prime minister in history to receive a permanent SEG escort.

The final decade of the twentieth century would see the longest recession for over thirty years, three overseas wars commanding the deployment of British troops, and the handing over of Hong King to China, which would mark the end of the British Empire. The 1990s would also bring a new vicious wave of terrorist attacks targeting the very heart of the capital. The security environment continued to surge, growing ever more international, unpredictable and sophisticated. Close cooperation with foreign security and police agencies grew increasingly important. For the first time, SEG officers would find themselves sent overseas to train foreign escort teams. Foreign officers from all over the world would visit the UK and become temporarily attached to the SEG for basic training. Not only did this give officers from different countries the opportunity to share best practice, it also helped align working practices and behaviours so when the foreign protection teams visited the UK they were properly prepared.

Resilient, defiant, and damn right determined to keep calm and carry on, the British public powered on through years of terrorism and global turmoil. There was the beginning of the Gulf War and Operation Desert Storm, the end of the Cold War, the collapse of Yugoslavia, as well as two Balkan wars in Bosnia and Kosovo. British involvement in these high-profile conflicts meant possible retaliation in the UK could not be dismissed. Due to their activity in the 1980s, the perceived threat of Middle Eastern groups mounting attacks on UK soil was high, although by the turn of the century we would learn that the greatest danger continued to come from within our own borders.

The IRA had failed to reach its ultimate objective – to bring the British government to the negotiating table, forcing them to agree to the establishment of a republic and the reunification of Ireland. Many of the IRA's political leaders were to reach the conclusion that an additional line of violence was required. As the bombing of political and military targets continued, a new campaign was launched, which was aimed at the economy and critical infrastructure. Airports, railway stations, the underground system, buses, tourist hot spots, pubs, shopping malls, popular shops and stores as well as banks and business hubs were all under threat. Before 1990 was out, roughly ten IRA bombs had exploded in London, with many more deterred or disarmed by the security forces. On 20 July of that year, a bomb ripped a ten-foot hole in the London Stock Exchange, although thankfully no one was injured. 'If the purpose of this callous act was to bring the City to a halt, they have failed singularly; our systems and services have functioned perfectly, and trading has continued as normal,' said Andrew High Smith, Chairman of the Stock Exchange.

By the end of the decade there would be hundreds more. On 7 February 1991, the IRA successfully landed a homemade mortar shell in the rear garden of 10 Downing Street just metres away from where the prime minister was attending a cabinet meeting. Recently installed armoured glass deflected the assassination attempt.

Fewer than 7,000 people would call the square mile home, but with over 500 banks setting up base within its boundaries, the City of London had become the world's most important economic trading ground. More than 300,000 workers flocked to their City offices on a Monday morning and there was continuing growth, economic stability and secure operating conditions. The IRA's tactic was to topple those conditions, disrupt the flow of business, instil fear into those who worked in the financial services industry, and gain a stranglehold over the economy. Causing millions upon millions of pounds of damage, the London Stock Exchange, Baltic Stock Exchange and

Bishopsgate were all to fall victim to the campaign. Similar attacks extended outside of the City boundary. Most notably, on 9 February 1996, the end of a seventeen-month ceasefire was marked by a hugely-destructive bomb blast in London's second financial district, Canary Wharf in the Docklands.

With the SEG now responsible for safeguarding the transit of Bank of England assets on a regular basis, all attack scenarios had to be planned for. It was clear that transits would be an attractive target for the IRA. A successful hit would achieve the desired economic harm, as well as damage confidence in the British security architecture in an area where the public would expect it to be at its strongest.

## The Decision to End Precision

In the first two years of the 1990s, a handover of senior management responsibility for the SEG resulted in it being moved from the traffic division to the Commissioner's Office (Territorial Operations) before arriving at its final stop – the Royalty Protection Operational Command Unit.

After forty years, the group had taken flight and landed in a new nest in the organigram. The senior management debate preceding the decision as to whom the SEG should belong was no doubt contentious and it was contested by some. However, as the group's role in providing mobile protection to members of the royal family had increased, the argument was put forward to home it in an environment of likeminded officers with similar roles and responsibilities.

The relationship with Royalty Protection was already very good, so joining forces with the SEG caused few ripples. 'Initially few noticed our arrival; it was basically a paper exercise,' explained one officer. 'The impact to us operationally was minimal. Perhaps the biggest change was to the shoulder numbers on the officers' uniforms.'

Nevertheless, it wasn't long before the impact of settling under Royalty Protection was felt. By the end of summer 1992, the MPT was to conduct its last display at Lippitts Hill (then home to the Police Firearms School and Air Support Unit). Despite two of the group's most experienced officers putting forward a compelling and well-constructed argument to retain the team, 'senior management had decided to close us down on the grounds of finance,' explained a member. Those wielding the axe also claimed that the high demand for the SEG meant that there was little time for team shows.

It could be said that the precision team formed a nucleus for the group until it was made permanent. The showbusiness nature of the MPT commanded immaculate presentation for the crowds, and both this attention to detail and the precision developed and perfected in manoeuvres, became part of SEG's day-to-day work. Over the years, the team delivered hundreds of displays before thousands of individuals: an achievement of which the SEG was very proud.

The MPT's popularity at public fairs had always been unrivalled. As one officer explained: 'The Mods and Rockers would turn out to many of our displays. At the end of the show, the Rockers would often come over and tell us how good we were.' During the 1960s the MPT had even travelled overseas. Perhaps the most noteworthy of the foreign adventures was the team's participation at the International Police Exhibition at the *flugplatz* (airfield) in Hanover, Germany, as recalled by PC Ray Young:

'The motorcycles were sent ahead of us in an articulated lorry and we travelled by boat and train. We'd loaded the motorcycles into the lorry using a crane, but when we arrived in Germany all we could find was a long, wooden scaffolding plank. We carefully rolled the bikes down the plank one by one. It turned out that we'd opened the sealed lorry before customs had conducted their checks and they nearly impounded all our bikes. Luckily Jock Shields was able to explain and clear things up for us.'

Spare bikes and even a police mechanic had travelled to participate in the exhibition. During the stay the team was invited to conduct a ride before tens of thousands of people at Hanover Football Stadium. 'Despite having just won the World Cup against West Germany, the crowds still cheered and gasped as we did our cross overs,' said Ray. 'At the end of the show one of the spectators jumped over the barrier and came to thank us, saying how wonderful it was to see a British police unit in Germany.'

The MPT was an important part of the SEG's history and a great source of pride, but while its closure had been a sad loss, it didn't come as a total surprise. The 1990s had seen a new climate of financial scrutiny and anything but essential frontline policing activities was slowly eroded away. Streamlining would have its benefits in modernizing the police, but closing the team entirely was perhaps short sighted. With hindsight, it would seem the decision failed to acknowledge the full value of the team. Not only did the MPT provide an excellent platform for public relations – including helping raise tens of thousands of pounds for charities every year – it was also an opportunity to maintain, practise and enhance SEG tactics. The freestyle format of team training days allowed officers to reach a level of precision riding that the standardized motorcycle courses at the police driving school didn't. The MPT's popularity and crowd-pulling ability also helped promote knowledge and awareness of a broad range of policing issues, not just those relating to road traffic safety.

## STT – Seriously Tough Training

Building on four decades of experience and the continued improvement of dedicated protection courses, training would continue to professionalize and intensify. The heightened terror threat level commanded a much more comprehensive approach to training than before. In addition to a full complement of advanced car and motorcycle certificates, officers also trained in advanced convoy tactics (driving very closely together at high speed) and prepared for various hijack scenarios. They also had to attend and pass various Royalty Protection and Special Branch bodyguard courses.

Realizing that officers needed to be competent drivers of the widest range of vehicles, they were required to obtain a PCV (Passenger Carrying Vehicle) licence. When time permitted, familiarization vehicle training would also take place in cooperation with the fire and ambulance services, as well as the military. To allow them to usefully assist in the event of an injury, officers were also trained in advanced first aid. There were even courses on rehearsing and coordinating actions between the SEG and military mounted units such as the Household Cavalry. New recruits would complete training within the first six months. From the early 1990s onwards, all officers, no matter how experienced, would undergo regular refresher training on all skill sets. In addition, high levels of physical fitness were expected of all officers, and routine tests ensured that standards were met. A gym was built into the basement of the SEG garage to reflect the new fitness order.

'Firearms training for members of the group had initially taken shape in a standard weapons course and they were trained as Authorized Firearms Officers – AFOs,' explained Dave Tilley, a retired firearms training officer who was attached to the SEG for three years. He explained how it changed:

> 'In addition to becoming an AFO, SEG had to attend tactical refresher training which had been especially designed for their duties. By the early '90s we'd trained them on Heckler and Koch MP5 carbines to give them greater firepower. This meant that they no longer needed the Specialist Firearms Unit to back them up on high-risk prison escorts.'

Unlike many of our European neighbours, Britain has adamantly resisted routinely arming the police. The British police, therefore, take the responsibility of arming their officers extremely seriously. Firearms training is as much about teaching officers a particular mindset as it is about showing them how to fire a weapon accurately and safely. The police's firearms doctrine places an emphasis on engaging a firearm as a last course of action, and only when there is a clear and immediate threat to life. In such instances officers may have to make snap decisions, sometimes based on very little information. In the case of the SEG, firearms would most likely only be drawn if under ambush, and in such an event it is more than likely that the attacker would be heavily-armed and well rehearsed. Training days are designed do their best to replicate such scenarios. The meticulous observation and intense coaching can put students under significant pressure.

To help lighten the atmosphere on training days, instructors would occasionally throw out a few well-placed jokes as well as the odd practical prank. Dave Tilley recalled that 'one morning a group of SEG officers dropped by our office for a short training visit before heading off on one of their local runs.' As usual they left their four motorcycles and a Range Rover neatly lined in the private parking area. 'Back then they had a stick-on metal sign attached to the rear of their vehicles which said "Special Escort"', said Dave. 'I switched it for one that said "Ford Escort". I understand it took several hours before someone noticed.'

Training, no matter how well designed or delivered, should never be a replacement for a willingness to learn from everyday routine business. The SEG understands this and one of the factors that contributes to its continued excellence is without question the group's enthusiasm for what is termed the 'post mortem'.

## Post Mortems

It has been proved that the most highly effective teams in any field are those which share a common culture of willingness to learn from mistakes. There are three aspects to a useful lesson-learnt process – what worked, what failed and what can we do differently next time? However, it's important to remember that in some cases, what worked or didn't work, might work for someone else or work for the same person under different circumstances in the future. The process works at its best when it becomes instinctive and second nature – a routine habit.

Having received the tradition of post mortems from the MPT, the SEG officers went about perfecting the process, asking those three questions after everything they did. It's fair to say that this self-evaluation was on their mind before, during and after every run. As a matter of tradition at the end of each run, officers rally together and verbally walk backwards through events to see if something could be learnt. As the following example depicts, honesty is a must. A name, blame and shame culture isn't allowed, but contributors to the debate are expected to be forthright in both giving and receiving feedback. Why do they bother? Because they see the immediate benefits of the change it brings, and in some scenarios, they know that someone's life could depend on it.

On a routine run, the easy rider – in this case a team leader – found himself approaching a busy central London crossroads without the support of a leapfrogging escort. Each of the three constables who comprised the escorts was far behind the convoy, trying eagerly to catch up. Having no other choice, the easy rider was forced to stop at the red lights (it's not a first choice as a stationary target is an easy target) and wait for the escorts to control the junction ahead. At the end of the run, the team leader called the escorts over for a quick post mortem, 'What happened there then?' he asked. 'Where were you, and why weren't you in place at the junction?'

Following much finger pointing and raised voices from the escorts, the team leader realized that the fault was in fact almost entirely with him. He had not kept a slow enough pace, and had taken several unexpected turns, which resulted in the convoy following a different route from normal. This had meant his teammates, who were leapfrogging between junctures, had to work harder than the pace of the convoy would allow. 'Have you had your say?' asked the team leader. The constables nodded looking worried, obviously beginning to regret the dressing down they'd given their supervisor.

'Follow me', instructed the team leader and together they rode to the nearest police canteen where he offered them 'bacon sandwiches and a cup of tea on me'. With the dust settled, and now in a more familiar setting, they talked through a series of small mistakes and misjudgements that had led to the convoy being caught out at the traffic lights. In doing so, each realized that he could learn and improve for the next run. On this occasion, it turned out that no one was specifically to blame; rather it was a fault in their methods, which they now knew how to correct. Summing up, they all agreed that 'we learn routines, not routes – and that's what keeps us working as a flexible team.'

## Royal Relationships

*Heaving crowds look on cheering, cameras flash from all directions, and the paparazzi push and shove desperate for a headline image. You settle down into the rear passenger seat of the limousine placing your handbag to one side. As ever, you keep your composure. Looking ahead you see reassuring eyes in the mirror – your police driver. He provides a light-hearted update of an incident from earlier which makes you chuckle. Your protection officer, sitting in the front passenger seat, offers you a smiling glance then gives a signal for the escort to proceed. As the vehicle gently pulls away, the noisy crowd is left behind. The easy rider, who you think you recognize, is sat just inches away from the nose of your vehicle. Picking up speed, two motorcycle escorts pass by silently either side of the car. You had kept your cool for public and the press, but seconds before entering the vehicle your heart was racing and a headache was coming on. Now you're able to unwind. You know you're in safe hands.*

*As you take another deep breath you notice the scent of a favourite fragrance. One of the officers has placed a tiny tissue inside the vehicle's air vent doused in perfume. You love your job, you're good at it, and you wouldn't change it for the world, but there are so few opportunities to be alone, to think or to reflect. Your mind is still racing and you need to focus. You remind yourself to slow down and in your mind you hear the words of an experienced aide: 'The prize is in the moment not at the finishing line.' Experience has taught you to take advantage of the minutes of peace as and when they come. You think about making a long-overdue call to a loved one but you pause. For the briefest of moments, you close your eyes and think ahead to your next appointment. You're attending the opening of a new charity. When you arrive, you'll be placed into the spotlight – again surrounded by people and with your every movement and every word under observation.*

*A binder of papers sits next to you tied with a purple royal ribbon – waiting patiently for your attention. You still need to read over your speech. Looking*

*at your watch for a moment you worry about arriving late. The pavements are*
*bustling with pedestrians and the roads are busting with vehicles. Your car is*
*about to reach a busy set of traffic lights and the signal has just turned red. Damn.*
*But one of your escorts is already there, holding back traffic so you can progress*
*through. As you pass he gives you a polite nod and you return with a smile. You*
*laugh inwardly at your earlier concern – you're never late when you're with your*
*boys. For now, you can rest.*

*Now just a few minutes away from the venue, you remember that a guest at the*
*previous event had spilt red wine on your dress. The schedule has been so hectic*
*you'd forgotten all about it. A spare dress is lying in the boot of the car but there*
*won't be a time or place to change when we arrive at our destination. You speak*
*to your protection officer: 'Toby, erm, I don't know how to put this but I need to*
*change my dress before we arrive at the charity ball.' It turns out that Toby had*
*noticed the stain and had already crafted a solution. Once more you can relax.*
*They really do think of everything.*

'On the whole, interaction with the royals was always on a professional, albeit very friendly, basis,' explained a SEG officer. 'It was rare that you'd have a personal conversation with them, but occasionally that would happen.' One such occasion was when a team of three escorts arrived early parking up outside Thatched House Lodge, a royal residence located in Richmond Park. It was a Saturday morning and the VIP, Princess Alexandra, came out ten minutes ahead of time and struck up a conversation with the officers. 'This sort of thing happened from time to time,' said an escort who was there. 'If an officer was ever injured on a royal escort there was always an enquiry as to the individual's condition from the respective member of the royal family.'

Lying by the side of the kerb, bike wrecked, pride punctured and bones broken, the last thing the officer expected was for Princess Diana to come and sit with him, but she did. It was a precious few moments for him and gave an insight into her caring personality. His concentration had wandered for a split second and he'd fallen off at speed whilst progressing towards a set of traffic lights. He'd lost traction on kerbside gravel and then slipped on a large patch of oily diesel. An accident of this kind, remarkably rare for the SEG, was almost entirely unavoidable. I say 'remarkably' rare because the routine manoeuvres would result in countless accidents if copied by even the most competent of normal drivers. 'Almost' being the optimal word, because the group share a firm belief that nearly all accidents are avoidable with the correct road position and situational awareness.

When the officer arrived at hospital, rumour of his regal roadside carer had already reached the doctors and nurses, as one former colleague recalled:

> 'Later that day two of us went to visit our wounded teammate to check up on his progress. When we arrived in the ward, his bed was surrounded by medical staff. At first, we thought something serious had changed in his condition. This was surprising since he only went in with a broken arm and bruised pride. Being experienced traffic officers we knew that internal trauma could be hard to spot in the first instance. Fearing the worst, we jogged over to the crowd. Reaching his bedside, we soon realized the staff weren't at all worried about his medical condition. He was fine. Rather they were quizzing him about the princess.'

On another occasion, following a similar accident concerning a different officer, Princess Diana paid him an unannounced and unexpected private visit, spending half an hour or so chatting with him by his bedside.

Just two weeks prior to this accident, a member of the royal family had visited the garage at Barnes to meet with the group. This wasn't the first of such visits. Indeed, royal calls on the SEG were virtually annual events and cherished by all. Although protocol was strict, the visits would take place in a relaxed, cheerful atmosphere. The usual format was for the visiting royal to be shown around the garage and then introduced to the civilian garage staff who were responsible for maintaining the vehicles. This was followed by an inspection of the motorcycles, cars and Range Rovers. Sometimes the royal would sit on a bike or climb into one of the police cars and practise their radio chatter. They were then taken upstairs to meet with the remaining civilian office staff, who were in charge of the office paperwork and whom the SEG considered to be the rock on which daily operations were built. The visit would normally conclude with a traditional group photo of all

SEG staff sitting on tiered benches with the royal visitor sat in the middle of the bottom bench.

---

*October 30th 1987*

*Dear Chief Superintendent Winglesworth,*

*I just wanted to write to say how very much we all enjoyed our visit to the Special Escort Group on Tuesday. I have always been an admirer of the way the motorcyclists operate, and am always so grateful to always arrive on time – sometimes in the face of what appear to be impossible odds. It was a real pleasure to meet the people who make it all possible.*

*William and Harry could hardly believe their good fortune in being allowed to play with real motorbikes, and will wear their uniforms with pride (in Harry's case for years to come!).*

*Do please pass on my sincere thanks to Inspector David Prout and all his team for their kindness. It was a lovely visit and I look forward to seeing them in action again before long.*

*Yours sincerely*

*Diana, Kensington Palace*

---

Perhaps the most discussed, and for many, the fondest of all the royal visits to the garage was by Prince William and Prince Harry together with their mother, Princess Diana. The boys were just five and three at the time and all reports suggest they found the experience to be rather wonderful. Legend has it that the boys had been asking to meet the 'friendly policemen on bikes' for many months and finally, their wish was granted. On arrival, they were met by one of their favourite policemen and taken straight to the fun area – the basement. Both were pictured sitting on a BMW motorcycle wearing specially-made SEG uniforms, gauntlets and helmets. Diana, who is said to have held the SEG in great esteem, often wrote to officers privately to thank them for their work, and even occasionally called up on the phone to check up on individuals or simply just to have a chat. It was clear that Diana was eager that her children would get to know the group well. Both boys went on to become avid motorcyclists. Officers confirm that one of them, and we won't say which, is an extremely competent and accomplished motorcyclist.

The relationship between SEG officers and members of the royal family has always been one of total trust and mutual professional admiration. Their work commands it. Members of the group gain a unique insight into the lives of royalty. They witness private moments and overhear personal conversations. The royals know that this confidence will never be broken. It's not about national secrecy; it's about common decency. In turn, the royals understand and value the work of the SEG. They know the hard work and the commitment that goes into keeping them safe, they recognize the group's skill and they appreciate the danger the officers face by offering them protection.

## Meeting the Monarch

The opportunity to stand face-to-face and exchange words with Her Majesty is a rare thing even for those who work with her daily. As a constitutional monarch, she no longer has a political or executive role. However, as the longest-reigning monarch in the world, she has overseen thirteen prime ministers, meeting with each of them in private on a weekly basis. For many of those prime ministers, she has provided invaluable advice.

As one might imagine, her diary is exceptionally busy. She has, on average, attended eight state visits per year either in Britain or overseas, with each spanning a period of four to five days. She receives hundreds of dignitaries and meets with thousands of people annually, and even in her tenth decade she carries out around 300 official engagements a year. She has attended over 15,000 official engagements since become Queen.

Over the years, members of the group have received private notes from Her Majesty, often thanking them for their help, or perhaps wishing them well on their retirement. Composing such a message is by no means a matter of protocol; rather it is at the whim and discretion of the author. As one might expect, such correspondence becomes a treasured possession. But interactions aren't restricted to letters.

Despite her many commitments, HMQ's personal staff will often request that select members of the group rally together in the palace quadrangle. Out of sight from the public eye, they will line up their motorcycles and stand neatly by their side ready for inspection. Such occasions are a daily occurrence for HMQ but a once-in-a-lifetime moment for the invitees.

It is a tradition set by HMQ herself and the honour is shared between all members of the group.

As guests of the royal household, officers are treated with a great deal of courtesy and respect. Household staff offer friendly and helpful pointers on how to address the Queen, assist in getting the officers into position, and make suggestions to ensure the meeting goes well. As one officer recalled:

> 'We were stood lined up waiting for Her Majesty. Hours had been spent polishing our bikes, tucking away loose wires and hiding radio cables so as to make them look as smart as possible. We knew the Queen wasn't very keen on our whistles. She preferred us to keep a low profile and remain as quiet as possible whilst we were at work escorting her. One of the household staff suggested we tuck the whistles well out of sight. We normally had them hanging from our tunics. Smart and well prepared, we were ready to meet HMQ.
>
> 'Her Majesty slowly walked along our line asking questions and thanking us for our work. First in line I smiled eagerly and exchanged a handful of polite words with HMQ. She moved along the line and I glanced at my fellow officers. The last officer in the line had forgotten to hide the whistle, which was hanging from a silver chain attached to his breast pocket. On sight of the instrument, the Queen said: "Ah, so you're the one that blows that loud whistle?", to which he responded: "No Ma'am, I'm the one who forgot to hide it from you." She chuckled with a sparkle in her eye.'

Exchanges between members of the royal family and their guests at these sorts of inspections are often light hearted and brief. However, sometimes conversations can be direct or more personal. On one such occasion officers were again lined up outside the palace for a similar inspection, but this time the Queen had something pressing to discuss. 'We should have noticed something was up when the household staff requested a supervisor from the group to attend,' explained one of the officers in attendance. 'When the Queen materialized from the palace she walked briskly up to my colleagues and asked: "Which one of you decides the routes?" "I do Ma'am," declared the supervisor.' What the officers didn't yet know was that her chauffeur had complained about a route the group had opted for the previous week. 'The Queen continued: "If you went out to Walthamstow, which way would you go?"'

Before answering, a thought ran through the officer's mind. The then 70-year-old lady standing before him had spent her entire life living in central London, and for over sixty years she had been ferried about across the capital. Intelligent and extremely astute, it was likely she had a good knowledge of London's backways and byways. Selecting his words with care he said: 'All the one-way systems leaving London are in your favour, so subject to any known traffic delays I'd select the most direct route.' The Queen pressed on: 'And how would you come back?' Having not expected her questioning to continue, the officer took a short breath before answering. 'I wouldn't come back that way Ma'am,' he said, 'I'd come back through the East End.' 'And would you go as far as the Docklands?' asked the Queen. 'Yes,' he said. 'That would be a good route. All the roads are set for coming back into central London. I'd probably take the convoy along the river.' In a slightly elevated voice, the Queen responded by saying: 'I think that's probably a long way round', to which the officer replied: 'Well it wasn't me anyway!' She then moved on to speak with the other officers but fortunately for them the discussion had come to an end. Point made.

Although they see her on a regular basis, personal interactions with HMQ create cherished memories for all the group. As one retired officer explained, sometimes the smallest of silent connections would become the most memorable:

'We were taking the Queen to Windsor Castle and en route we became stuck in traffic and were sat still for several minutes – a rare thing but sometimes it does happen. Preparing to move off, I manoeuvred my bike so it was aligned to HMQ's passenger window. The traffic was still not moving, so I glanced through the side window of the Rolls Royce only to see the Queen looking up at me smiling inquisitively. I shrugged my shoulders and she smiled back. That moment will stay with me forever.'

## VE Day Celebrations

As the pilot looked down from thousands of feet above, the sight of 250,000 people flooding towards the gates of Buckingham Palace was impressive.

They cheered as they looked up at his Second World War Fairey Swordfish torpedo bomber. Seconds behind him, lined up like flying dominoes, was a series of tactical fighters and bombers. As the Swordfish approached the palace, the crowds waved their Union Flags, creating an ocean of red, white and blue. All this synchronized with Her Majesty the Queen Mother, HMQ and HRH Princess Margaret walking on to the balcony to greet the crowds. As the day of nationwide celebrations came to an end, there would be a two-minute silence in memory of the millions who lost their lives. The evening concluded with over 1,000 beacons spread around the coastline of the UK to commemorate the allied victory.

Riding up from Cheltenham, PC Martyn Hillier was en route to London. An officer with Gloucestershire Constabulary, he'd been handpicked by colleagues at the SEG to help escort during the VE Day celebrations. As soon as the operational orders landed on his desk he packed his panniers and set off. Martyn was a trusted colleague and friend of the SEG. An experienced traffic officer and expert motorcyclist, he'd fitted in like a hand in a gauntlet to the methods and techniques of the group. He had first encountered the SEG a year earlier when he and a handful of his colleagues started to provide regular escorts to members of the royal family visiting their Gloucestershire country residences. However, he and his team lacked expertise. 'I felt that we were inadequately trained for our new duties and wanted me and my colleagues to learn from the best,' explained Martyn. 'I contacted the group and we were soon invited to London and gained valuable insights into how they work. They were every bit as good as we thought they were.'

On arrival at Hendon Police College, Martyn attended an operational briefing together with approximately 150 police officers from across the Metropolitan Police Service, the City Police and the Royal Parks Police. The college would be his home and base for the next five days of operations. Well over 100 heads of states, foreign ministers and other dignitaries would be attending the VE Day weekend commemorations, with each of them requiring an escort. It was a massive project to coordinate. Now attached to the SEG, Martyn, together with two regular group members, had been assigned the prestigious task of escorting the Prime Minister of New Zealand, Jim Bolger. 'The PM was staying at the Sheraton Hotel in Knightsbridge,' he recalled. 'We'd been given a busy programme to escort him over several days. All journeys started at the hotel.'

On the first day, they were to escort him to Lancaster House to attend ministerial meetings, then to Buckingham Palace to have lunch with HMQ, before going to St-Martin-in-the-Fields to attend a memorial service of for a New Zealand war hero, and finally to 10 Downing Street for a meeting with Prime Minister John Major. Martyn and his two SEG colleagues would also do a recce of each of the runs in advance. 'As a West Country lad not overly familiar with London, this was mostly for my benefit,' he said.

Waking to the 4.00 am alarm, Martyn began getting ready. He and his colleagues, who were travelling in from different parts of London, were to assemble at Heathrow Airport to meet with the PM's plane at 6.00 am. 'Just as I was about to leave Hendon, a message arrived from the Foreign Office stating that an escort was no longer required,' he said. However, the message hadn't got through in time to one of the other officers so he continued his journey to the airport. This was lucky, because when he arrived it was discovered the Foreign Office had made a mistake. 'My colleague would have had to conduct an escort designed for three on his own,' Martyn added. The day went off without a hitch and he even got a photograph of himself outside No 10. The programme continued over the next few days without any more hiccups and PC Hillier received invaluable on-the-job SEG training to take back to Gloucestershire. The penultimate run with Prime Minister Bolger was to St Paul's Cathedral, where he was to attend a memorial service. 'We then took him across the Thames to Waterloo Station where he and several other heads of state joined the Eurostar for Paris where they would join in further commemorations.'

A good job done, Martyn had participated in an event worthy of mention on his already very impressive CV. 'After the drop off at Waterloo, it was back to Hendon for lunch and then on to the M4 for my journey home for a good night's sleep,' he said. His performance during the VE Day commemorations was noted by his SEG colleagues as 'exemplary, meeting all the standards expected of a member of our group.' Several years later, when close to retirement, PC Martyn Hillier was to be recognized for his contribution to motorcycling and road traffic safety with the Queen's Police Medal (QPM). The QPM, is given for gallantry or exceptional distinguished service. He had done the SEG proud.

## Nelson Mandela's State Visit

'The time for the healing of wounds has come. The moment to bridge
the chasm that divides us has come. The time to build is upon us.'
Nelson Mandela's inaugural address as President of South Africa

As he stood before tens of thousands of his citizens to mark the beginning of
his presidency, Nelson Mandela hoped that this would be the end of racial
segregation in South Africa. Of Thembu royal descent, he was born into a
country governed by apartheid enforced by a white minority. Giving his life
to a struggle for equality, and turning to political extremism and sabotage,
Mandela was imprisoned from 12 June 1964 until 11 February 1990. From the
constraints of his cell, Mandela continued to lead the struggle, saying 'ideas
cannot be silenced by prison walls.' In 1996, two years after his appointment as
president, Mandela would find himself in the UK at the invitation of HMQ.
A self-acclaimed anglophile, Britain had always played an important role in his
life. His first visit to the UK took place immediately after his release from prison
where he'd met with thousands of British supporters at Wembley Stadium.
The official state visit took place in London between 9 and 12 July 1996.

'Nelson was to be provided with all the trimmings of a full state visit,'
recalled PC Peter Skerritt, who worked on his escort. 'This included a
ceremonial escort, which is spectacular and extremely complicated but looks
fabulous when done properly.' The formation was as follows: three bikes
form an arrowhead at the helm of the convoy and the middle bike works
as the easy rider. These are followed by the presidential vehicle, which has
a further seven bikes, one on each of the car's wheels, and three following
closely at the rear. The presidential vehicle is followed by a protection
vehicle. Depending on the speed of the convoy, the width of road and if any
junctions need to be controlled, the formation changes shape elegantly, with
the bikes manoeuvring around the vehicle.

Perfecting the formation required concentration. If the convoy were
to approach a busy junction that needed controlling – such as a set of
major traffic lights – the two bikes either side of the easy rider (currently
forming the arrowhead), would pull ahead to control the junction before
the convoy passed through. As this movement happens, all the remaining
bikes would move forward one position simultaneously. This means that the

bikes previously sitting on the front wheels of the presidential car were now either side of the easy rider at the helm of the convoy, once again forming an arrowhead. Once the convoy passed the traffic lights, the two bikes left behind to control them catch up and rejoin at the rear, taking up the empty position. All this is done in a synchronized fashion and with minimal disruption to the VIP. 'We always turned off our blue flashing lights and avoided revving our engines when passing the presidential vehicle,' explained Peter.

Mandela's programme was packed and he was met by ecstatic crowds at each appointment. On some occasions, it would take over ten minutes before the hordes would calm down enough for Mandela to begin his speech. One of his most important appointments was to take place at Brixton Community Centre where he would meet with Prince Charles, together with thousands of local residents. Brixton's police inspector had expressed concerns about security at the event. Although he expected everything to be peaceful and friendly, he believed that, in the event of a disturbance, the community centre would be significantly under policed. He also noted that there were insufficient crowd barriers outside the building. Despite voicing his concerns to senior officers, the event was to go ahead as planned.

'One of the Queen's own beautiful Rolls Royces had been loaned to Mandela for the duration of his stay [and] Prince Charles was to arrive at the community centre in a separate vehicle,' explained Peter. Once both Mandela and Charles had been dropped off, their cars were turned around and parked outside the main entrance ready for their departure. The prince was to return to the palace and Mandela was due to attend a meeting at the South African Embassy in Trafalgar Square. The Rolls Royce was in the lead, followed by its back-up car, then the Jaguar and back-up cars used by Prince Charles. 'We left the easy rider sitting in front of the Rolls while the rest of us formed up just around the corner ready to encircle Mandela's car on its departure,' recalled Peter. Four of the bikes formed into a square box. 'The remaining bikes, of which I was one, positioned themselves ready to deal with the initial junctions.' With the time nearing for Mandela and Prince Charles to depart the community centre, the crowds, as predicted, swelled enormously, with everyone wanting to catch a glimpse of the special guests emerging from the building. 'As Prince Charles was saying goodbye to Mandela at the door of the Rolls Royce, a huge crowd surged and enveloped the cars,' said Peter. 'It was all very friendly but far too close for the safety of the VIPs.' There was little choice but to bundle Charles into the Rolls Royce next to Mandela. 'As the driver of the Rolls moved off, the car was damaged by the sheer weight of the crowds. A mounted officer on his horse tried to assist in extracting the vehicles, but in the end only the Rolls made it out of the venue towards us.'

The Rolls Royce drove into the area prepared by the bikes and the convoy moved off at a slow pace. Regrettably, explained Peter, several of the protection officers, who ought to have been inside the VIP vehicles, had been left behind: 'It quickly became apparent that they weren't going to catch us up anytime soon since the officers were now on foot chasing after us.' Deciding to make for a place of safety, the convoy leader radioed ahead and planned for the vehicles to stop at nearby Kennington Police Station. The bikes had now caught up. 'The sight of this will remain with me forever,' laughed Peter. 'Several protection officers, including two from South Africa, and Prince Charles's own bodyguard, perched and dishevelled on the back of our single-seater motorcycles!' As luck would have it, the convoy would soon meet with a traffic police car, which one of the officers flagged down so the pillions could jump in. 'My job now,' explained Peter, 'together with a colleague, was to race ahead and prepare Kennington Police Station for an unplanned VIP arrival.' This he did and as they entered the station yard, his colleague homed in on a PC who'd helped him prepare the yard for the vehicles. 'I went straight into the police station to find a senior officer.' An inspector from the control room came skipping down an internal flight of stairs to greet him. 'Our eyes met and I recognized him from earlier in my career. He looked very pale and just asked: "Is it true?" I said "Yes, you'd better say hello." At that moment both Prince Charles and Nelson Mandela had exited the Rolls Royce and were walking towards us.'

Leading the two VIPs into the police station, Peter noticed how Nelson Mandela seemed completely unfazed. Mandela was closely followed by Prince Charles, who approached Peter and said 'I've seen it all now. My man on the back of one of your bikes!' Soon after the rest of the vehicles caught up, regrouped and the convoys continued as originally planned.

At the end of the state visit, Peter and his colleagues presented each of the two South African protection officers with an SEG tie. 'These ties are only to be worn by those who have performed a royal escort on a bike', explained Peter. The South Africans were delighted.

Princess Diana's Funeral
Escort

## The Funeral of Diana, Princess of Wales

It was an accident that shocked the entire world. Diana, Princess of Wales died in the early hours of the morning from injuries caused by a tragic high-speed car crash. The accident happened at the entrance of the Pont de L'Alma road tunnel on 31 August 1997. News spread across the world in a moment – a moment that would be remembered by billions forever.

Princess Diana's funeral was held at Westminster Abbey on 6 September 1997, watched live on television by more than two billion people around the world. Over thirty-two million people in the UK alone watched the event unfold (one of the highest viewing figures ever). More than one million people lined the streets of London in order to pay their respects.

The first part of the funeral began at Kensington Palace. The coffin, placed on a horse-drawn gun carriage and covered by the Union Flag, was transported from the palace to Westminster Abbey, escorted by a foot patrol of the Queen's Guards, together with members of the Metropolitan Police Mounted Branch. Over 500 representatives from charities supported by the princess walked behind the cortege.

Following the ceremony at Westminster Abbey, the coffin was placed into the rear of a black Daimler hearse. The vehicle then proceeded slowly along a closed route, lined by steel barriers, and foot patrol police officers.

Twelve officers from the SEG were grouped to escort the princess on her final journey. The team sat waiting outside the Irish Embassy in Chapel

Street on the junction of Grosvenor Place. PC John Swain, communications officer was sitting in SEG Range Rover and when he gave the signal, the group moved up Park Lane and towards the south side of Marble Arch.

Forming into position, the group was ready to receive the hearse. In place of the conventional police high-visibility jackets, each of the officers was dressed from neck to toe in black uniform as a mark of respect. Each one wore identical gloss-white, closed-faced crash helmets and sat proudly on a new gleaming white BMW R1100 motorcycle. Each of the bikes had been built to the unique specifications of the group. The dealership had moved heaven and earth to get the fleet of bikes released early so they could be used at the funeral.

'The bikes moved into position forming a box in which the hearse would enter,' explained PC Swain. When the hearse turned the corner into Marble Arch, it rolled gently into the centre of the motorcycle formation. With the hearse slowing pace, but not stopping, the bikes skilfully lifted off. The movement was incredibly elegant. 'The front of the box, comprising three bikes, was shaped as an arrowhead,' said PC Swain, 'The remainder of the box was formed by four motorcycles, one sitting on each of the wheels of the hearse.'

'Two bikes, sent ahead of the cortege, were appointed green and red diamond, to act as a visible warning to the police on the ground of the impending arrival of the escort,' added PC Swain. The final three motorcycle escorts followed ten minutes behind the cortege escorting a spare hearse – in case the first one broke down.

The hearse travelled the two-and-a-half-hour journey to Diana's childhood home, Althorp, without family. The princess's own family were travelling on the royal train. She was now in the sole care of the SEG, a team whom she, and her children, had grown to know well. It was a team she was extremely proud of, and whom she referred to as her 'brave boys'. One retired officer recalled the emotion of the day:

'Diana visited us at our garage a number of times. Both her sons, Prince William and Prince Harry, as young boys, had also spent time with us at Barnes. It was an incredibly emotional experience for all of us who were involved in escorting her cortege. None of the officers knew her on a personal basis, but her way with us was always friendly, thoughtful and often inquisitive.'

PC Bob Stewart, who had taken the position of 'wheel man' during the escort, said 'the Daimler, carrying the princess's coffin was then closely followed by an SEG Range Rover, housing a further three officers. My initial impression was how old the hearse was. I wondered what would we do if it broke down.' Sergeant Tony Dolan, who had ridden at the point of the arrowhead, recalled his feelings at the sight of the hearse: 'I had a quiet thought to myself. You're in safe hands now. You're with us. I also felt angry. If she'd been looked after by us this wouldn't have happened.'

The cortege departed Park Lane. The route was heavily policed by foot patrol officers, who were helping to keep the huge crowds on the pavements and away from the road. Slowly the number of officers reduced, and the crowds spilled out on to the street. The crowds were heaving with energy and emotion. Hundreds of bunches of flowers were thrown at the passing hearse, many landing on its roof and bonnet. I asked PC Stewart if this had nearly caused an accident and he said:

> 'The flowers weren't a problem, although when they hit you on the head it could be a bit distracting. The main problem was the cellophane wrapping, which was spread out all over the road. Avoiding it would have made the bikes look messy, so there were moments when the bikes twitched a bit as they slipped over the plastic.'

At one point there were thousands of people blocking the way ahead, and the crowds either side of the cortege were closing in, leaving only the thinnest of gaps to pass through. As a consequence, the box formation was adjusted slightly, gently manoeuvring the motorcycles to sit ahead of, and directly behind, the hearse, rather than on the vehicle's wheels. This made the cortege thinner and less likely to collide with a pedestrian. The change in formation was done so elegantly, the alteration was barely noticeable. 'The first time it happened I thought, God, what were we going to do?' admitted PC Stewart, but he needn't have worried. 'We could see where we were going and the crowds were obviously aware we were approaching. As we grew close to them they would move back, and the road would miraculously open up for us.'

One of the most vivid moments of the escort was when the hearse came to a stop near Staples Corner on the M1. 'A pile of flowers had landed on the bonnet of the hearse,' explained PC Swain. 'They needed to be cleared before moving on to the motorway and increasing our speed. I radioed the helicopter I99 and asked if they could find a safe place for us to stop. They suggested the start of the M1.' As the cortege came to a stop, PC Swain confessed that 'there was a horrible moment when I thought the attendant of the hearse was going to throw them to the side of the road. But he didn't. He laid them down with due reverence.'

As the cortege moved off and progressed up the M1, Sergeant Dolan remembered how 'the motorway looked like a desert. I'd never seen it like that – completely clear.' But that wasn't to last. Within minutes, hundreds of people had found their way to footbridges and the motorway sidings, rambling across fields and footpaths to reach their destination.

The cortege was to travel through several police jurisdictions before arriving at Althorp House where the princess was to be buried on a small island inside the private estate. 'Chief constables of the constabulary areas that the escort passed through tried to argue a case for their officers to take over the escort at their force boundaries,' said PC Stewart. 'The discussion only lasted a brief moment, as a directive came from high – very high! – that the SEG would perform the entire escort.' This directive, however, wasn't to prevent the forces from participating and showing their respects. 'Numerous police cars, motorcycles and ambulances from the various police counties formed up along the side of the M1,' he recalled. 'There were even dog handlers and mounted officers.'

When the cortege arrived at the gates of Althorp, the bikes stopped and the hearse continued into the grounds. 'We stopped for a moment while the gates were closed,' recalled PC Stewart, 'I remember taking my crash helmet off, and looking down to find a rose trapped between my leg and the petrol tank of the bike. I kept it, took it home and my wife pressed it as a memento which we've kept to this day.'

Having completed their duties, the officers quietly grouped together and began their journey back to the garage. Sergeant Dolan had mixed feelings as he and his colleagues rode away from the burial site: 'We'd said our final farewells,' he said. 'Although it was a sad day, I was happy because we'd done our job well. But I was also disappointed; the biggest day of my police service was over.' On the way back to London, the group decided to take a short break at services on the M1. 'We'd parked our motorcycles outside the service station entrance and lined up neatly, as we normally would,' recalled PC Stewart.

'Following a quick visit to the facilities inside, we returned to our bikes where a growing group of members of the public had gathered, complimenting my colleagues on the work we'd done that day. It was a lovely moment.'

Every second of the funeral, and the escort, was recorded and televised live from hundreds of cameras. The most iconic images were captured from a helicopter circling above. Those images are of the SEG, closely formed around the flower-covered hearse. 'The escort was without doubt a defining moment in modern history,' added Bob Stewart. 'It was the media event of this century, with live pictures broadcast around the globe. This of course served to enhance the already high reputation of the SEG.'

## Our Youngest VIPs

Perhaps one of the reasons Princess Diana had such a fondness for the group was due to its charitable support. Over the years, the SEG has helped raise hundreds of thousands of pounds and assisted in placing the spotlight on some very important causes. One of those charities is called Dreamflight, an organization that helps change young lives by taking seriously ill and disabled children on the holiday of a lifetime to Orlando in Florida. The group has supported Dreamflight since its first flight in November 1987, when the SEG escorted Princess Diana, who was waving the excited children off on their trip. 'This is where our relationship with the group also took off,' explained the charity's founder, Patricia Pearce MBE. 'It has always been a privilege and pleasure working with them. The skill and precision of the SEG motorcyclists is really quiet something to watch.'

Every year since then, Dreamflight has flown a group of deserving children to America for their dream holiday. At the initiative of the SEG, and to the delight of the charity, it was suggested that the children might find it fun if they were given a police escort from their hotel to the airport. This wonderful tradition has continued and now, every year, a small team of SEG motorcycle officers join the children first thing in the morning. They sit talking with them as they have breakfast and the staff are preparing them for their flight. In recent years, the Metropolitan Police dog unit has also joined the youngsters for breakfast – bringing in puppies for them to play with. The officers even help serve the breakfast to the children and crew.

A few moments before the children leave the hotel, the SEG officers return to their bikes and rally around the buses. As the children are ushered out of the hotel the first thing they see are the SEG officers sitting on the bikes, now wearing their police jackets and white helmets. And there's more. Each of the officers decorates their motorcycle elaborately with Disney toys, Mickey Mouse ears and lots of teddy bears. 'As you can imagine the children really love this,' laughed Patricia. 'As the coaches head off, and the officers get to work escorting us to the airport, the children are full of smiles, laughter and giggles watching them out of the window.'

As the coaches arrive at the airport they are taken directly into a hangar where their aircraft is waiting. The children embark the plane and the SEG officers sit on their bikes, lined up next to each other, waving them goodbye. What a wonderful way to start a holiday of a lifetime.

## My role with the SEG

I had just turned 19, had recently finished school, had no chance of going to university, and had not yet decided whether to join the armed forces or the police, when I secured a part-time summer job at a water garden and tropical aquarium centre in the golden mile at Crews Hill, north London. The cycle to and from home took about two hours of my day. I didn't consider it a burden since I knew my fitness would need to be good for whatever future career picked me. Both of my brothers and my granddads had served in the armed forces, with my middle brother then serving as a commando in the Royal Marines. Meanwhile, I'd failed my exams at school and somehow ended up catching tropical fish and cleaning out dirty tanks. The job was fun, at times educational, and occasionally rewarding, but I couldn't see myself staying there for very long.

Then along came a welcome disruption to my summer forecast. My dad, who had recently retired from the SEG, was hired by the Metropolitan Police to help organize a huge workforce to assist with the Asia Europe Conference to be held at the Queen Elizabeth II Conference Centre (QE2) on 3 and 4 April 1998. The conference was a gathering of heads of states and government officials from ten Asian and fifteen European nations under the chairmanship of Prime Minister Tony Blair. Dad asked me if I'd like to help out and the answer was a very clear yes. He responded by saying 'wear a nice suit'. I'd already spent several days with the SEG at the garage and on the national bodyguards' training course so I was excited to finally see them at work in a real-life situation. On my first day, I drove in with Dad from our home in north London. Our base for the next three days was a redundant London bus shelter located directly behind Victoria Station. As we walked into the massive enclosed space there were hundreds of police and emergency vehicles lined up around the perimeter of the building. A long queue of uniformed officers was being processed to receive the daily orders. There was another more popular queue leading to a table full of styrofoam cups of tea and coffee as well as bacon sandwiches wrapped in paper: 'the staple diet of a bobby,' an officer told me later in conversation. I joined that queue.

Looking around I could see a few familiar faces. One of them, a police constable appointed to my dad's team, came over to me placing his arm around my shoulder saying: 'I've got just the job for you Chris.' I was expecting to be handed a bucket of soapy warm water and a sponge but what actually materialized was far more exciting. Along with some instructions, he handed me a mobile phone, the first I'd ever held, and told me to call a number that he'd written for me on a small piece of paper. The man at the other end of the mobile was a recently retired Royal Marine who'd served in the elite Special Boat Service. After leaving, he'd set up an events security company together with some of his former colleagues, specializing in event security. Receiving my orders, I went and stood outside at the agreed rendezvous point. I wasn't waiting long before a black Jaguar, escorted by a single police motorcycle, arrived flagging me to jump in. I couldn't believe it. This was incredible and ridiculously cool. Minutes later the escort dropped me off at an anonymous-looking portable building, which was propped up in one of the private carparks running alongside the Mall. Climbing into the cabin, I opened the door to find a very fit looking man in his early forties – let's call him Jim – flicking through maps whilst speaking on a handheld radio. Looking directly at me with a serious face he waved me in and pointed to a chair. I sat down.

From what I could surmise, the radio conversation pertained to a suspicious vehicle parked close to the QE2. Jim stood up from his chair, shook my hand, and said: 'Chris, come with me, we're heading over to the conference centre.' Minutes later another Jaguar arrived but this time without a motorcycle escort. During the short drive to Westminster, Jim explained what he needed me to do. My task was to write down all the number plates of suspicious-looking vehicles parked along the streets immediately surrounding the QE2 building. This was the day before the conference and every precaution was being taken.

As we pulled up outside the centre, Jim invited me to jump out pointing in the direction of a uniformed police officer who was stood waiting for me. The police officer handed me a notebook, pen and a handheld radio, and off I went.

During the following two days, I made my own way to work taking the London Underground and reporting in for duties at the bus station behind Victoria. They were long days, starting at Victoria around 7.00 am and finishing in the early evening, but they passed by as quick as a flash. Although I was only escorted once, I saw the SEG at work dozens of times as they ferried various heads of state to and from the QE2. I'd also gained a unique insight into the world of security operations, having spent time working with both military and police experts, getting a feel for their culture, and an insight into how they think and behave. I'd discovered my dream job.

**BMW K100 (1990-1997).** As the collaboration between BMW and SEG matured, a motorcycle tailored to the specific needs of the group was developed. Many former members of the group will say that the K100 was the best of the escort bikes. The four-cylinder engine produced 90bhp. The upright riding position, elegant looks and cleverly-balanced design offered an accurate ride. The new addition of paniers, which contained essential equipment, were designed especially narrow to assist the rider manoeuvring through tight gaps in traffic. Less chrome to polish than on previous bikes, but the grooves between the fairing detailed in black looked very cool.

# The Future

Weather-toughened and carefully honed through sixty-five years of intense experience, the Metropolitan Police has developed a sophisticated protective security capability, which embodies the SEG as its core. In six and a half decades of service, and with several thousand high-profile and high-security runs under its belt, it has, almost without exception, delivered its charges safely, uneventfully, and on time (an accolade no foreign security team of its kind can claim). As one retired inspector in charge of the SEG put it: 'I used to receive letters every month from foreign security teams telling me how my officers were the best they'd ever worked with. I was overwhelmed with requests to allow my officers to provide training overseas.' SEG's motto is spot on. The group is, unquestionably a world leader at what it does.

Having read the group's story, I suppose that many of you, like me, have experienced a spot of career envy. In that light, I have written what I imagine to be a fitting job advert, which I ask you to consider to see if it matches your suitability:

**We have your dream job – but are you our dream applicant?** The combination of operational complexity and a demand for total professionalism is in itself challenging. Not for the faint-hearted, you'll be expected to work at the sharp end of the Metropolitan Police Service's protective security team.

**Job satisfaction?** Your role couldn't be more rewarding – to protect world leaders from harm, and to ensure the safe delivery to justice of the UK's most dangerous criminals and terrorists. At the heart of history in the making, your job will ensure momentous moments unfold unhindered.

**Type of person?** We don't do types. We do teamwork.

**Competencies required?** You'll need all the aptitude and nous expected of someone who is responsible for escorting our monarch and mixing with presidents.

**Problem Solving?** We do our best to avoid them, but they do occur. So you'll need to demonstrate quick thinking and sound judgment in high risk and high-pressure scenarios.

**Mistakes?** It's how you recover from them and move forward that matters most.

**Mindset?** Disciplined, determined, conscientious and, no matter what your background, experience or skills, you should be good humoured (most of the time) and be willing to learn, adapt and advance.

**Training?** You'll learn how to use guns, motorcycles, high-powered cars and bodyguard techniques through intensive personal development programmes founded on decades of experience and delivered by the best across our community. You must be willing to accept constructive criticism as we expect you to be capable of giving it. You'll even get a personal coach for the duration of your time with us – we're all coaches to each other in the SEG.

Surrounded by something much more than a conventional team, you'll be supported, mentored and pushed to your best by colleagues who share an *esprit de corps* like no other. If successful in application, you'll be one of just a handful of individuals who have joined our family since our inauguration. With sixty-five years of uninterrupted and infallible history, you'll be joining a world-class team who need world-class individuals.

*You applied, and following interviews and tests, were found to be suitable. In fact, you were an exceptional candidate. Not surprising since you have several years of impressive experience behind you. As one of a handful of motorcycle surveillance officers, you have excellent knowledge of riding in central London. Former jobs required you to hold a firearms certificate, and several years spent in Traffic Division back in the late 1980s gave you all the skills needed to become a supervisor/team leader in the SEG.*

*Waiting for a position on the next SEG training programme, which is scheduled to begin in a few weeks, you are invited to visit the garage to meet your new teammates. Normally a recruit would have to wait several months for their background checks to be completed, but because of your former positions you already hold all the necessary paperwork. As you walk into the office, you're struck by the atmosphere. The corridors have a welcoming, cheerful vibe. It's clear that everyone here enjoys being part of the group.*

*You notice the walls of the corridor are covered with memorabilia from the group's long history, including hundreds of car flags from countries all around the world. You find out that these have been gifted to the group at the end of state visits and that the collection is officially registered as the largest of its kind in the world. Framed in the centre of the wall is a drone shot photograph of the group outside Buckingham Palace at the top of the Mall. Seen from above, the motorcycles form the number 90. The image was sent to HMQ on her birthday. Suddenly, a sense of huge responsibility washes over you and you almost need to pinch yourself. Not only does the team you've just become part of provide the highest level of security to the world's most important leaders, it's also been at the forefront of the country's most important ceremonial occasions since before you were born. Whether they were happy, sad, or solemn the SEG led the way for decades, helping events run smoothly – from the VE Day celebrations to the state visits of world leaders to the funerals of, amongst others, Sir Winston Churchill and the Queen Mother. It's hard to believe you're now one of the honoured few who will serve this most important function.*

*All practical and physical training now complete, you're nearly ready to go live on your first run. The final part of your induction is to attend a series of security awareness seminars. They will include briefings on known terrorist and criminal threats. The presentations are compiled by the intelligence community and presented by the Counter Terrorism Command (CTC), which was established following a merger between Special Branch and the Counter Terrorism Branch more than ten years ago. Surrounded by an audience of nearly 150 officers from across the Metropolitan Police, a young civilian analyst, maybe 25-years-old, walks up to the podium and begins her presentation. You learn about a diverse range of threats as the analyst provides case studies from the past.*

*Having completed all training, you're now in the group and your first day at work is spent away from the garage. Your first task is to attend an operational planning meeting at New Scotland Yard for the London Marathon. In former days, the group provided a ceremonial escort for the lead runners, but for budgetary reasons that task was handed over to a civilian company, which specializes in hiring retired SEG and protection officers. Senior officers are once again considering SEG involvement. A decision is deferred until further research is completed.*

*Back at the garage, you dwell on how training and technology has moved on so much. Your colleagues are teaching you unimaginably-advanced tips and techniques that are rightly and properly safeguarded from public consumption. With the rise of Islamic terrorism in the West, the security environment has altered considerably, forcing momentous changes to the way escorts are conducted. Astonished at the variety of runs the group now has, you're excited to see what the year ahead will bring. One of the biggest eye openers is learning that the SEG is a small part of a wider protection strategy, and that hundreds of others are involved behind the scenes across Royalty Protection and Special Branch. You're the legs and arms of the body, whilst others operate the eyes, ears, arms and head. It's both comforting and inspiring to know that when you're out on the road, you're supported by a sophisticated and well-trained team keeping the machine running smoothly, covering your back at all times.*

*Collecting scores of stories by the week, you've already shaken hands with several heads of state. There are about thirty of you in the team, each of you with a slightly different role and thus a slightly different perspective of the same day. There's never a dull moment; every one is memorable. You're left with too many stories to share and too many secrets to divulge. Having read this book before signing up, you realize much has changed. There is so much more to how the group operates. It's impossible to get it all down on paper.*

*Now six months into the job, you've gained experience and are familiar with the methods and routines. You also begin to realize that, despite all the changes, some things haven't changed at all since the early days. The dedication to precision motorcycling and the commitment to immaculate presentation are exactly the same as when the group escorted Marshal Tito in the 1950s. Although the garage now contains an electronic carwash, your colleagues insist on checking their bikes manually to ensure the best possible finish. Unlike in former days, when each officer was responsible for keeping their own motorcycle in good fitness, a team of mechanics now maintains your vehicle. Despite this, you check over its vital signs every time you start the engine. You're surrounded by some of the most advanced technology money can buy, yet no matter how intelligent the innovations have become, you must still shine your own boots, and you shine them well. The job still has the scent of engine oil and polish.*

*Before leaving the garage, you listen to the latest security briefing describing recent terrorist attacks in London. You think to yourself, the group has done well to resist the temptation of stepping on to the ladder of infinite securitization. Colleagues before you were able to battle and survive dangerous times because they retained agility. They were independent and free of external interference, and consequently they gained from the group's unique experience. The skill of your craft is based on much more than science, of staff selection, training, equipment and procedures. It's also an art, based on a unique culture and an incredible esprit de corps that cannot easily be quantified or accounted for.*

*You have a feeling it's going to be a good day. All checks complete, you climb on to your motorcycle and catch a glimpse of your name bag in the wing mirror – 'Eugenie' – destined for Buckingham Palace. You're about to escort the monarch, Her Majesty the Queen, for the first time.*

**BMW R1100RS (1997–2012).** An award-winning sports tourer in the US, the BMW was fitted with a powerful 1000cc boxer twin engine. Once again it was packed full of modifications especially for the SEG and the new ABS braking system was a welcome feature. President Bush senior was so impressed with his motorcycle escort that he requested to have his photo taken sitting on the lead SEG officer's BMW during an informal visit to the UK. This particular model of SEG motorcycle is perhaps one of the most publicly well known as it was employed during the funeral of Diana, Princess of Wales. The motorcycle was eventually replaced by a near identical 6 speed R1150RS.

Sandringham House

25th November 1988

To all members of the SEG,

I was so touched that you should have written as you did for my birthday. I still can't believe I have reached the somewhat ripe age of forty! What really worries me is that I must seem so ancient to my children. Hopefully they'll begin to think I'm a wise old man....! Thank you a thousand times for thinking of me. I do so appreciate it.

With every best wish,

Charles

## Letter from David Finnimore, Chief Superintendent Traffic Division

*Senior Security Co-ordinator*
Apart from routine policing operations, a number of officers have additional responsibilities in specific areas. One such area is 'Security Co-ordination'. This is a standalone role for special security events such as the State Opening of Parliament or State Visits from Foreign Dignitaries. Senior Security Co-ordinators ensure the various facets of the security operations work together and don't inadvertently create breaches, conflict or weaknesses in the overall plan they have designed.

The SEG were an invaluable resource and always a tactical option in providing appropriate security to events. The SEG remained one of the primary employment options to be considered. The skill demonstrated by the SEG was an exception to the rule. Everything from the way they mastered their own standard of police vehicle Roadcraft, right down to how they paint the manufacturer name on the walls of their tires with gold pen. The attention to detail is incredible.

The first operation was to facilitate the movement of the 200+ members of a wedding. The wedding involved most of the Royal Families of Europe including our own and as such presented a considerable target for the 'Mad, Sad and Bad' Brigade who thrive on the opportunity to disrupt, or worse, attack members of these households. Additionally, they represented a potential terrorist target which would have attracted any of the world's media who were not already present. The SEG were employed to escort (for escort read 'protect') the royal vehicles between venues including church and reception.

Having worked previously with the SEG I knew what I had bought into. Firstly, consummate professionalism in protecting, assisting and facilitating the movement of the vehicles carry the VIPs between venues. Secondly, and rightly, the external view available to both protected person and well-wisher of the importance and splendour of the event, given the SEG's unique motorcycles, precision riding and smartness. The event went without issue and was a credit to the service.

The second operation was to receive a foreign dignitary at Heathrow Airport. This person was to be accompanied by a large retinue of personal protection officers from that country. Despite agreements, which it has to be said do not always work or are complied with, some protection officers are not happy to remain under the eye of the host country and seek to avoid utilising the support offered. To this end the elements of the protected convoy became 'disengaged' from the escort. This could have serious consequences for HMG (and the MPS) should an adverse event befall it. I employed the SEG to search and re-establishing contact with the 'detachment'. Using motorcycles and an intimate knowledge of Heathrow and the environs, contact was made safely and with incredible efficiency, the escort group re-established itself. For my part I was conveyed by an SEG driver at a rate of knots I did not think possible for any standard saloon car in order to make a visual verification that all was now well. We have a great responsibility as the host country and the SEG had our backs on this occasion.

Overall I have always been proud to see the SEG in any policing operation. Their personnel and vehicles are always immaculate. Team work is demonstrated with every action from starting to stopping. But it is in the protection afforded by that employment we should praise and treasure.

**Honda VFR1200F (2012-present).** With its ability to accelerate a heart stopping 0-60mph in under three seconds and boasting a top speed of 157mph, the Honda is the quickest motorcycle ever employed by the SEG. The highly-adapted motorcycle, designed for the specific needs of the SEG, contains cutting edge technology. With a sharp and modern design, dressed in SEG livery, the bike has significant road presence. The riding position is stooped forward compared to previous SEG motorcycles which have a more upright posture.

**SEG Chiefs**
Arthur Tisdall (on a project basis 1952–1959)
Charles Day (1959–1963)
John Baldwin (1963–1973)
Derek Gosse (1973–1976)
Rick Johnson (1976–1981)
Martin Vaisey (April 1981–1983)
David Prout (1983–1988)
Jim Read (1987–1992)
John Gouldsmith (1990–2000)

**SEG Motorcycles (approximate dates deployed to the SEG)**
Triumph Speed Twin 5T (1952–1959)
Triumph Thunderbird 6T (1959–1967)
Triumph TR6 Trophy 'Saint' (1967–1980)
BMW R80/7 (1980–1990)
BMW K100 (1990–1997)
BMW R1100 – r1150RS (1997–2012)
Honda VFR1200 (2012–present)

# Index